pistachio

pistachio

savory & sweet recipes inspired by world cuisines

By Barbara Bryant & Georgeanne Brennan

Photographs by Robert Holmes

Design by Jennifer Barry

with contributions from celebrated chefs and food writers

CAMERON + COMPANY

Petaluma, California

CAMERON + COMPANY

149 Kentucky Street, Suite 7
Petaluma, CA 94952
www.cameronbooks.com

Publisher: Chris Gruener
Editorial Director: Pippa White
Creative Director: Iain Morris
Managing Editor: Jan Hughes
Editorial Assistant: Krista Keplinger

Library of Congress Cataloging-in-Publication Data available.
ISBN: 978-1-949480-31-3

10 9 8 7 6 5 4 3 2 1

Printed in China

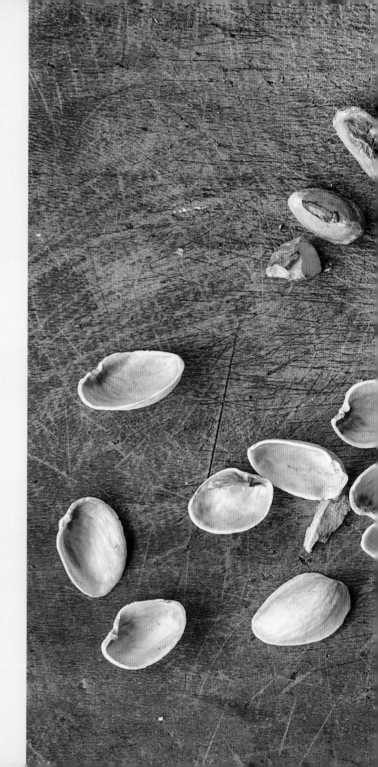

RIGHT: *Once shelled, whole pistachio kernels are coarsely chopped for adding to a variety of sweet and savory dishes.* FOLLOWING PAGE: *Rows of fifty-year-old pistachio trees are laden with nuts at Keenan Farms in California's San Joaquin Valley. The trees are over fifteen feet (4.5 m) tall.*

contents

preface

This is my third cookbook about nuts. You can imagine the jokes that family and friends continue to "crack" about my passion for them, yet I continue. Why? I'm captivated by their history, taste, botanical beauty, endless culinary uses, and portability. I love the idea that something so small can pack so much flavor, crunch, and nutrition. The tiny pistachio epitomizes these qualities.

All nuts are heavenly, but I find pistachios particularly divine. I've loved them since childhood. My parents, whose entertaining heyday began in earnest after World War II, always served fancy mixed nuts, and we children were warned not to eat all the little green gems from the bowl before the company arrived. Many years later, I remember the red-dye residue left on my fingers after eating pistachios. That was at a time when importers felt the need to improve the shell aesthetic to attract new customers.

Because of their size, nuts are eminently portable—easily tucked into pockets and satchels. In the past, this allowed migrating peoples to bring their beloved food wherever they traveled, not only as sustenance but often as barter and medicine. Today, pistachios can still evoke childhood memories for many immigrants whose attachment to the nut began long ago. From their beginnings in the Neolithic Age in the Middle East and central Asia to their cultivation in the English-speaking world, pistachios boast a noble past that makes me appreciate their taste even more. The fact that a pistachio tree can live up to three hundred years and tolerate extreme heat and drought is further testament to the nut's longevity.

Part of the fun in eating pistachios is wrestling them from their shells. (For any stubborn shells, just use an empty one to pry it open.) One of my sons lived on pistachios when he was growing up, a worthy substitute for popcorn, and he continues to munch on them while watching sports games on television. Despite their long history, pistachios still have an exotic feel to me, and I am eager to try any new pistachio product I see. Like wine, which reveals its terroir, pistachios grown around the world bear the unique and distinctive flavor and texture characteristics of their growing conditions. Sampling pistachios in all their forms and from various farms has helped me broaden my appreciation.

I've only recently started using pistachios in my cooking. I began by making pistachio butter instead of peanut butter, mixing the nuts in a food processor with salt, a little agave nectar, and olive oil. It's so easy and good. Often times it doesn't make it to the piece of toast it's meant for, and I eat it right off the spoon. It's a great little snack.

Pistachios are finally getting the attention they deserve. I am delighted to see how chefs throughout the country have brilliantly integrated and elevated the role of pistachios in their inventive recipes, from cocktail snacks to desserts, reflecting the popularity of this estimable nut in cuisines around the world. We are inspired to share these innovative recipes with you, adding our own renditions of traditional dishes with a modern twist. From their sweet to savory delivery, pistachios never cease to transport me to another time and place. We hope this book will have the same effect on you.

—Barbara Bryant

introduction

The history of pistachios is replete with colorful characters ranging from Persian kings, biblical luminaries, and Roman emperors to crusader knights, nut traders, and American plant explorers. The nut's human history begins around 7000 BCE in northeastern Iraq, where evidence of human consumption of the nut was found by archaeologists in the dig site of Jarmo, an ancient farming village. Native to what is now Turkey, Iran, Iraq, Syria, and part of southern Russia, the pistachio has found favor throughout the world, but it is still grown in relatively circumscribed regions that have hot, dry summers and cold winters.

Prized for its rich flavor throughout the Persian Empire and used not only whole and chopped for desserts but also ground for enhancing sauces and pressed for oil, the nut was introduced to ancient Rome by Emperor Vitellius in the first century CE, possibly brought to him by his father, Lucius Vitellius, who had spent time as a consul in Syria where it was prevalent. The nut gained popularity in its new setting, and with some help from Rome's conquering armies, it spread throughout the Mediterranean and as far north as England.

Pistachios gained a second culinary foothold during the Middle Ages. Christian Crusaders, who encountered the nuts while in the Holy Land and from traders along the Silk Road, reintroduced them to their homelands on their return from the religious wars. At the same time, Muslim settlers from North Africa introduced pistachios (among many other foods still dominant today) to Andalusia and Sicily during their eight-hundred-year reign.

FACING PAGE: *Clusters of ripening California pistachios in spring.*
RIGHT: *Botanical illustration of the pistachio plant, c. 1835.*

Pistachier en fruit

Borne of the Desert's Breath

Among nut trees, the pistachio is the most drought and heat tolerant. It is long-lived (up to three hundred years) and large, easily growing up to thirty feet (9 m) tall. This makes it an ideal nut-bearing tree in hot, dry climates.

When pistachios first evolved in high-altitude desert climates, they had little vegetation to harbor insects. As a result, this dioecious nut tree spread using wind to transport the pollen issued by flowers on male trees to flowers on female trees, which bear the nuts. Both male flowers (catkins) and female flowers (rachises) lack petals and nectaries, as they have no need to attract insects.

As a desert tree, the pistachio has developed multiple survival tactics, among them "alternate bearing," which is the ability to shed buds for the following year's crop during the year it is producing a heavy yield. The result is alternating high and low crop yields. The low year allows the tree to develop reserves to support the following year's crop and decreases the insect population by denying them a fruit host.

Pistachios are deciduous and require mildly cold winters for the male and female trees to bloom strongly and synchronously and for the females to be successfully pollinated. However, successful pollination does not always provide the twenty-five to fifty pounds (11 to 23 kg) of dry nuts per tree farmers hope to produce.

—LOUISE FERGUSON, PhD, University of California Davis
Department of Plant Sciences

Pistachios in the New World

It took centuries for pistachios to reach the New World, where the nuts were first imported in the early 1900s by newcomer immigrant merchants. Middle Eastern and Mediterranean natives who longed for their favorite foods in their adopted homeland quickly became the primary market for the nuts. By the 1930s, pistachios were a staple of American vending machines found in train stations, bars, and restaurants selling "a dozen for a nickel."

Although a seed distributor did bring pistachio seeds to California in 1854, preceding some trees that were imported to California from France a few years later, the pistachio did not stir commercial interest until the federal government sent horticulturist William E. Whitehouse on an expedition to Persia and Turkestan in the late 1920s. Whitehouse returned with samples of the best and hardiest pistachio seeds he found, and planted them in test plots at the US Department of Agriculture's recently established Plant Introduction Station in Chico, California. Of the seeds planted in Chico's hot, dry climate, one was deemed best for cultivation in California: the so-called Kerman, named by Whitehouse after the ancient Iranian city of Kerman, the capital city of Kerman Province, where he obtained the seed. The Kerman pistachio remains the major variety grown in California.

It wasn't until 1976 that California growers produced their first small commercial crop. The California pistachios were well received, but Iran dominated the market, producing tens of thousands of tons, which were exported all over the world, including to the United States. That changed abruptly in 1979 when the Iranian hostage crisis prompted the cessation of US trade with Iran. This was a dramatic turning point for US pistachio production. Today, the United States leads the world in pistachio production and exportation, followed by Iran and Turkey. Collectively, these three countries account for 90 percent of world production. California alone produces 99 percent of all the pistachios grown in the United States, making the state the world's largest producer of the popular green nut.

The pistachio had its inauspicious introduction to the Americas in 1854, when it came to California and was planted as a garden tree. Its path to domination, however, was instigated by the founding of the Plant Introduction Station in Northern California. In 1929, the station sent William E. Whitehouse, a deciduous-tree researcher, to modern-day Iran and central Asia on a mission to collect pistachio seeds for planting. According to botanical researchers at the University of California, Davis, that trip would result in the "single most successful plant introduction to the United States in the twentieth century."

Whitehouse returned to California with twenty pounds (9 kg) of different pistachio varieties. The station planted and studied three thousand trees, and within a few years, a single tree had succeeded beyond all the others. Sourced from the Agah family orchard in the Iranian province of Kerman, this star performer was given the name Kerman. Paired with a Peters variety male tree for fertilization, the Kerman would in time become the American pistachio. By the early 1970s, a number of California farmers had turned to pistachio plantings when water-dependent citrus and almond groves proved too costly to cultivate. The first commercial crop of American pistachios was harvested in 1976.

World politics raised the pistachio's profile dramatically in 1979 when a group of Iranian college students stormed the American embassy in Tehran, taking dozens of hostages. The resulting crisis soured relations between the two countries, and the American government slapped a 300 percent tariff on Iranian pistachios. A tongue-in-cheek *New York Times* story noted, "This California pistachio is brought to you courtesy of the Internal Revenue Service and the shah of Iran." Today, there are 950 pistachio producers in the United States, with California, Arizona, and New Mexico making up 100 percent of the country's commercial production.

—BLAKE HALLANAN, journalist

ABOVE: *(left) William E. Whitehouse in central Asia on a USDA botanical expedition, 1929; (right) Whitehouse surrounded by photographs of pistachios at the USDA Division of Plant Exploration and Introduction, 1951; photographs courtesy of Hunt Institute for Botanical Documentation, Carnegie Mellon University, Pittsburgh, Pennsylvania.*

World Production Areas

Successful pistachio production is limited to areas of the world that have semiarid conditions with long, hot summers and cold but not freezing winters. The Iranian plateau fits that profile, and pistachios have been cultivated there for thousands of years. Much of the production is in small orchards of only a few acres, but this is gradually changing. Southeastern Turkey, which includes the UNESCO Creative City of Gastronomy of Gaziantep, has ideal growing conditions for pistachios, and production there has been increasing due to new plantings, improved cultivars, and modern cultivation and harvesting methods. California's San Joaquin and Sacramento Valleys, where rain rarely falls between May and November and winter temperatures can drop to near freezing, are California's prime pistachio-growing regions.

PREVIOUS PAGE: *Pistachio orchards at Keenan Farms in California's Central Valley are irrigated by the California Aqueduct.* ABOVE: *The Keenan family and friends stroll through the family's fifty-year-old farm in Avenal, California.* FACING PAGE *(clockwise from top left) Pistachio orchards of the Santa Barbara Pistachio Company below the hills of the Sierra Madre range in California's Santa Barbara County. At Keenan Farms, large mechanized "shakers" grip pistachio trees and shake their trunks to loosen the ripened nuts, which are collected in a bin on the machine. In Iran, pistachios are both machine and hand harvested before loading into large trucks for transport to the processing plant. Pistachios are harvested by hand in the fertile land surrounding Mount Etna in Bronte, Sicily. Pistachio orchards line the undulating steppes in Gaziantep Province, Turkey. Harvesting pistachios is a family affair on a small farm in Turkey.*

World Pistachio Production

The United States, Turkey, and Iran continue to produce over 95 percent of the world's pistachio crop. The United States has been the top producer for the last seven years except for 2017–18, when Iran led production. In 2022–23, the US produced 55 percent of the crop, followed by Turkey, Iran, Syria, and Greece. Other EU production comes mainly from member countries Spain and Italy. California alone produces 99 percent of the US pistachio crop. The 2022–23 world production was recorded at just under 729,000 metric tons.

United States	55%
Turkey	25%
Iran	15%
Syria	3%
Greece	1%
Others	1%

Other regions of the world meeting these growing conditions are found in Syria, Australia, Mexico, North Africa, South Africa, and the European Union (EU) countries of Greece, Spain, and Italy. In some of these countries, such as Syria, Italy, and Greece, pistachio orchards have been a feature for centuries, while in others, including South Africa, Mexico, and Australia, the plantings are relatively new. In Afghanistan, where pistachios grow wild in pistachio forests that are open and free to all, the people collect the nuts and sell them. However, all these countries together produce only a very small quantity compared with the harvests of the United States, Turkey, and Iran. Of these other countries, Syria and the EU nations currently rank fourth, fifth, and sixth in world production, still only a fraction of the output of the top three producers.

All pistachio trees are alternate bearing, meaning that every other year they set a small crop followed by a large one, further impacting yearly production amounts. Global warming is becoming a significant factor in the production of pistachios. Some countries, such as Mexico and South Africa, are looking toward increasing plantings of drought-tolerant trees as climate change makes growing traditional crops less sustainable.

In Mexico, where humans began domesticating corn around nine thousand years ago, farmers are finding higher temperatures and diminished rainfall a challenge to the traditional crop and are turning to pistachios as one alternative to corn. And in California, with continued years of drought and agricultural water usage severely curtailed, pistachios have become a major nut crop because of the low water consumption the tree demands compared to other nut-bearing trees. Together, changing climate and the growth in pistachio consumption are contributing to the increase in pistachio production in both major and emerging markets.

FACING PAGE: *Harvested nuts fall from the trees into large mechanical arms on the shakers at Keenan Farms.*
ABOVE: *In western South Africa, pistachio trees at the farm of Karoo Pistachios grow near the Orange River, not far from the small town of Prieska in Northern Cape Province. Photograph courtesy of Gitte Müller.*

Soil and Planting

Although pistachio trees will grow in most soil types, sandy loam is preferred because it allows the trees to sink deep roots, helping them to produce strong, healthy branches and tolerate drought. In newer orchard plantings, including almost all of those in California, the trees are planted twenty feet (six meters) apart to allow for mechanical harvesting. In the older, traditional plantings of Iran, Turkey, and elsewhere, the trees were planted closer together, making modern mechanical harvesting impossible. Because pistachio trees require a pollinator, male trees, which do not bear fruit, are interspersed with the female trees at a typical ratio of one male to every eight to ten female trees.

Pistachio Life Cycle: From Bud to Harvest

Pistachio trees start bearing at about five years, take up to twenty years before they reach their mature bearing period, and can continue to bear for another fifty to eighty years. The tree is wind-pollinated, and one male tree is needed for every twenty-four or so female trees.

In winter, the trees are dormant and the branches bare. During the seasonal cycle of the trees, regardless of cultivar—and there are many—the buds break in early spring when the trees come out of their winter dormancy. It is during this period that adequate water, whether by irrigation or rainfall, is required to ensure young growth and fruit development. The fruits develop in large, grape-like clusters that hang from the trees, with each cluster containing thirty to fifty nuts. As summer progresses and temperatures climb, the seeds swell, naturally cracking the shell, while the outer husks remain intact. As harvesttime approaches, the husks change from greenish yellow to pale or sometimes deeper pink, depending on variety.

PREVIOUS PAGES: *(left) Bare pistachio trees in winter at Keenan Farms; photo courtesy Teresa Keenan. (right) Farmer Richard Grotjahn with a handful of pistachios from his small farm near Davis, California.* FACING PAGE: *(clockwise from top left) A branch with female pistachio buds in spring; male pistachio buds. An orchard worker at Keenan Farms inspects newly formed nut clusters in late spring. As pistachios ripen, they develop a beautiful red tinge. Grower Grotjahn prunes his orchard in early summer. A newly ripe pistachio kernel is revealed inside its split outer shell after removing the reddish exterior husk.* FOLLOWING PAGE: *Orchards at Santa Barbara Pistachio Company.*

The hot days of late summer, typically from the end of August through September, depending on variety and geography, are harvesttime. Timing the harvest correctly and acting quickly are essential to a crop of quality nuts. If premature, too many of the nuts have not naturally cracked open, which is the desired stage. If left too long on the tree, the hulls begin to deteriorate and stain the shells, which damages the optimum quality of the nuts.

Harvest techniques vary around the world. In California, the nuts are machine harvested using shakers with mechanical arms that grasp the trunk and shake it for several seconds, until the nuts loosen and fall into a catch frame, which delivers them onto a conveyor belt. From there, they are moved into bins and trucked to facilities where they are mechanically hulled. Extended contact with the hull after harvest can stain the nuts, which is a serious marketing defect. Once hulled, the nuts are washed and dried and then sorted.

ABOVE: *A view of the pistachio processing plant from the orchards of third-generation California pistachio grower Keenan Farms.*
FACING PAGE: *(clockwise from top left) Harvested nuts are hauled by bulk harvesters and transferred by conveyors into trailers. After transport to the processing plant, the nuts move to float tanks that separate closed-shell nuts from open-shell nuts. Closed-shell nuts float in the tanks, and open-shell nuts sink. Each type undergoes further processing and is mechanically washed and dried before moving to a sizing machine. Once sized, the nuts move by conveyor for sorting by hand for quality. The nuts are finally loaded into giant sacks and stored to await shipment. Each sack weighs twenty-two hundred pounds (1,000 kg).*

In areas where hand harvesting is still practiced, workers go into the orchards. At orchards where the trees are low to the ground, workers pick the nuts from branches, filling buckets strapped to their backs. In other instances, they climb the trees to cut the nut-heavy clusters, releasing them onto mats placed under the branches. Sometimes, rubber mallets or other instruments are used to "shake" the tree trunks, causing the nuts to fall. The nuts are then loaded into trucks and taken to processing plants where the hulls are mechanically removed. Before the advent of processing plants, the nuts were hit with mallets and the husks removed manually, nut by nut. Once hulled, the pistachios are washed and spread to dry outside on cement slabs, where they are diligently watched and turned over for a period of two to three days until completely dry. Then they are sorted.

Bronte, in northeastern Sicily near Mount Etna, is home to more than seventy-four hundred acres (3,000 ha) of pistachios grown in volcanic soil between jutting lava flows. The famous Bronte DOP (Protected Designation of Origin) pistachios are highly valued for their brilliant green color, flavor, and high oil content. The volcanic soil where they are cultivated is rich, but the terrain is rocky, making mechanized harvesting impossible. Thus, harvesting is done by hand, as it still is in parts of Iran, Syria, and Turkey.

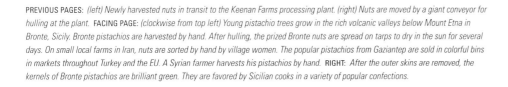

PREVIOUS PAGES: *(left) Newly harvested nuts in transit to the Keenan Farms processing plant. (right) Nuts are moved by a giant conveyor for hulling at the plant.* FACING PAGE: *(clockwise from top left) Young pistachio trees grow in the rich volcanic valleys below Mount Etna in Bronte, Sicily. Bronte pistachios are harvested by hand. After hulling, the prized Bronte nuts are spread on tarps to dry in the sun for several days. On small local farms in Iran, nuts are sorted by hand by village women. The popular pistachios from Gaziantep are sold in colorful bins in markets throughout Turkey and the EU. A Syrian farmer harvests his pistachios by hand.* RIGHT: *After the outer skins are removed, the kernels of Bronte pistachios are brilliant green. They are favored by Sicilian cooks in a variety of popular confections.*

Pistachio Trees in the Wild

Pistacia terebinthus, commonly called the terebinth, is a pistachio species native to the Mediterranean region. Often called the "wild" pistachio, it grows as a modest-size tree or large shrub and produces small seeds in a soft shell. The tiny, dark green fruits, called *çitlenbik, menengiç,* or *bıttım* in Turkish, are used in a variety of ways. They are much favored roasted as a crunchy snack (çitlenbik) or ground to make a mock Turkish coffee (menengiç kahvesi). They are also pressed to extract oil used in the making of traditional bar soaps (bıttım sabunu). Young shoots are gathered to make pickles that are consumed as a meze or added to salads to give them a pleasant briny taste.

Another wild pistachio tree, *Pistacia lentiscus*, produces an aromatic resin when the bark is incised. Interestingly, only trees that grow on the Greek island of Chios and around the Turkish town of Çesme, which lies just four miles (7 km) across the water from Chios, produce the resin. Named *mastic* in Greek and *sakız* in Turkish, it has a flavor much appreciated in milk puddings, ice cream, confections, baked goods, and liquors and is also combined with a little beeswax to make a sweet-scented chewing gum.

—AYLIN ÖNEY TAN, cookbook author of *A Taste of Sun & Fire*, food writer, columnist, and NTV radio broadcaster of *Bitter, Sweet, and Sour* in Turkey; www.aylinoneytan.com

Cultivars

There are hundreds of pistachio cultivars—along with wild varieties—scattered throughout the pistachio places of origin in today's Middle East and central Asia. Additionally, researchers are continually experimenting and developing new varieties with a view toward various desirable characteristics, such as early or late ripening, pest and disease resistance, and productivity. Different cultivars have different sizes and shapes as well.

In Iran, one of the most commonly planted cultivars is Fandoghi, which produces a round nut. The long, thin Ahmad Aghaei is also widely grown, while Akbari, a new, super-long variety, is gaining popularity. In the United States, Kerman, the original variety brought to Chico from Iran in 1929, continues to dominate production, but new cultivars, such as Golden Hills and Gumdrop, are being planted as well. Turkey's cultivars are indigenous to Turkey and are different from the Iranian strains. More than half of Turkish production yields long, slim nuts that come from two varieties, Kirmizi and Uzun, grown in the Gaziantep region of southeastern Turkey. The other major variety is Siirt, a round type grown in Siirt Province, also in southeastern Turkey.

Production and Economy

The value of the 2022–23 global crop is estimated at $6 billion. Worldwide production varies from year to year depending on each country's total production in a given year and in part because pistachios are alternate bearing. The largest producers are also the largest exporters. In 2022, China consumed 18 percent of the exported crop, while Germany alone accounted for 13.7 percent. Germany is also a re-exporter, primarily with sales to other EU countries. Italy is both a producer of pistachios but also an importer. Along with Turkey, India, and Vietnam, the four countries combined imported approximately 18 percent of the exports. Although Mexico only imported about 1.15 percent of the exported crop, that was an increase of more than 85 percent over previous years (prior five-year average). That market is expected

FACING PAGE: *Wild pistachio trees on the Greek island of Chios are prized not for their nuts but for their mastic, an aromatic resin produced from the trees' bark. It is used to flavor a variety of popular foods and beverages.*

to continue to grow, as is the EU market. The driving forces behind the increases in the EU appear to be the European interest in healthy snacks and a willingness to explore new flavors in both snacks and confections.

The US pistachio market has expanded the global market for pistachios with flavors such as chili, sea salt and vinegar, rosemary, garlic, and lime in snack packs and mixes, much in the same way consumers worldwide became enamored with intensely flavored potato chips decades ago. Pistachios are also having a surge of popularity in retail confections such as scones, candy bars, tarts, and cookies, and on menus nationwide as diners become more familiar with and interested in them.

Another source of the growing popularity of pistachios in the United States and Europe is the increasing appreciation of and interest in the foods and flavors of the Middle East, where the green nut has been both a prized and an essential ingredient for thousands of years. Celebrity chefs, cookbook authors, and television food shows have been enthusiastically extolling the virtues and diversity of the foods and flavors of the Middle East. This media exposure has been instrumental in introducing Americans to the flavors and uses of many of the region's foods and spices, including pistachios.

Nutrition

Among nuts, pistachios are the lowest in calories at 159 calories per ounce (28 g), less than half the amount found in the same-size serving of walnuts. With only 13 grams of fat per ounce (28 g), and 90 percent of those unsaturated or healthy fats, plus being rich in vitamin B6, potassium, and fibers, pistachios stand out as a healthy food. They are also high in antioxidants, as are walnuts and pecans, which fight the free radicals that can be responsible for a range of ills, from early aging to cancer and heart disease. Pistachios are also good for your vision because of high levels of lutein and zeaxanthin, which help to protect against macular degeneration and damage from blue light. So pistachios not only taste good but are also good for us—in moderation, of course.

Healthy Pistachio Power

Nothing gives nutrition professionals more pleasure than recommending foods that are both rich in essential nutrients and irresistibly delicious. Pistachios top the list for daily healthful snacking and for enjoying in dishes both savory and sweet. Nutrient dense but lower in calories than almonds, cashews, peanuts, pecans, and walnuts, pistachios have more protein than many nuts. A handful of pistachios—or about fifty kernels—provides as much protein as an egg and more fiber than an orange. Protein and fiber satisfy hunger, providing lasting satisfaction. The fiber also has a positive effect on the gut by aiding good bacteria.

The high levels of unsaturated fatty acids and potassium in pistachios have antioxidant and anti-inflammatory benefits, making them an excellent snack for brain health and for keeping blood sugar, blood pressure, and cholesterol in check.

Beyond providing healthful noshing, pistachios have a sensual balance of texture and flavor, making this friendly nut the one to reach for first. Their distinctive flavor profile and personality make them easy to include in wholesome, nourishing meals.

— ROBIN KLINE, registered dietitian and certified
culinary professional who has written widely on
food and nutrition topics for the *Washington Post*,
Cooking Light, and *Better Homes & Gardens*

Selecting and Storing Pistachios

Pistachios are available in many forms in the market, but the primary categories are in shell and shelled. The choice depends on how they are intended for use. In-shell pistachios are a popular snack item, and it's fun to let people shell their own nuts. If the nuts are to be used culinarily, it's more convenient to buy them shelled and ready to use.

For in-shell pistachios, look for unstained, ivory-white shells that are naturally cracked open. The kernels inside are fully mature and can easily be shelled by hand. Closed shells indicate both an immature kernel and a shell that will be difficult to open. In-shell pistachios are best stored in airtight containers in the refrigerator, where they will keep for up to a year, or in the freezer, where they will keep for up to two years. If kept unopened on a cool, dark pantry shelf, they will keep for up to six months. However, once a package is opened, pistachios should be stored in an airtight container in the refrigerator or freezer.

Shelled pistachio kernels, which are typically referred to as nuts, are naturally covered with a thin, papery skin that can be easily rubbed off after blanching (see page 42). Their size will vary depending on whether they are small, immature nuts or larger, mature ones. It will also vary by variety. Shelled pistachios are more expensive by weight, but you are paying only for nuts, not the shells. Store them in the same way as in-shell nuts but for shorter periods. Keep them refrigerated for no more than about six months and frozen for about a year.

As with all nuts, exposure to heat while stored leads to rancidity, which is the degradation of the nuts' natural oils, causing a bitter taste and off-flavor. If stored in the freezer, thaw before using. Thawed pistachios can be refrozen without any deleterious effects.

Toasting Pistachios

Toasting pistachios, either on the stovetop or in the oven, brings out the nuts' inherent flavor and intensifies it. The nuts also become crunchier, adding texture to whatever dish they are used in. The time and temperature for toasting pistachios depend on whether they are in shell, shelled, whole, or chopped. If you are toasting a relatively large quantity of nuts, oven toasting is the best method. Stovetop toasting is ideal if toasting only a handful or so, whether in shell, shelled, whole, or chopped. If the nuts are whole and in shell or shelled, heat a dry frying pan over medium-high heat. Add the nuts in a single layer and toast, stirring frequently and watching closely so they do not burn, until fragrant and lightly browned, 3 to 4 minutes. Remove from the pan and let cool or not as desired.

Chopped

If the nuts are chopped, they will toast quickly, making the stovetop method the preferred choice. Heat a dry frying pan over medium-high heat. Add the nuts in a single layer and toast, stirring frequently and watching closely so they do not burn, until fragrant and lightly browned, 1 to 2 minutes. Remove from the pan and let cool.

Whole, Shelled

Preheat the oven to 350°F (175°C). Line a sheet pan with parchment paper or leave it as is. Spread the nuts on the pan in a single layer. Do not crowd them. Place the pan in the oven and toast, stirring once or twice, until fragrant and lightly browned, 5 to 8 minutes. Remove from the pan and let cool completely.

Whole, In Shell

Preheat the oven to 350°F (175°C). Line a sheet pan with parchment paper or leave it as is. Spread the nuts on the pan in a single layer. Do not crowd them. Place the pan in the oven and toast, stirring once or twice, until fragrant and lightly browned, 8 to 10 minutes. Remove from the pan and let cool completely.

Pistachios in the Kitchen

Pistachios are one of the most versatile nuts in my pantry. Their natural sweetness makes them the perfect addition to almost any dish, savory or sweet. I think we all fall in love with pistachios in the shell as a snack because they are fun to open and addictive. But for many people, that is where their knowledge of the nut ends.

You can purchase shelled pistachios and prepare them in countless ways. I often roast pistachios with olive oil, salt, and chili powder to add to salads or to use as a crunchy topping for a pasta dish. Recently, I candied some with a little egg white and sugar to use on top of a strawberry and mascarpone dessert. Stealing from the southern tradition of boiling peanuts, I decided to get crazy one day and boil some pistachios to make a puree. The results were amazing, and I ended up using it as a filling for ravioli. I have also used it in place of tahini for hummus, and that, too, was delicious. I have never stopped eating pistachios as a snack, but they have become so much more to me and are indispensable in my home kitchen and at my restaurants.

— GERARD CRAFT, executive chef and owner
of Niche Food Group

The Pistachio Pantry

In recent years, as pistachios have increased in popularity, they have become more readily available in markets. Where once shelves held only in-shell raw nuts, now you can purchase shelled or in-shell nuts, raw or roasted, salted or not, or seasoned with a variety of flavors.

Store-Bought Pistachio Products

Pistachio products have surged in availability, too, as people have learned of the nuts' health benefits and have come to appreciate their nutty, slightly sweet flavor. Pistachio milk, cream, and oil are all now regularly carried on store shelves.

• Pistachio milk has a delicate flavor and is excellent whirled into smoothies, poured over breakfast cereals, and frothed into a lovely, airy foam for lattes. It can also be used in baking, but be careful not to overheat it, as its delicate flavor will be lost, and it will curdle. Note that some brands include sweeteners and can contain other nut milks and/or additives. For pure pistachio milk, look for brands that list only pistachios and water.

• Pistachio paste, also known as pistachio cream, typically contains 50 to 70 percent pistachios combined with dry milk, sugar, and other ingredients to create a sweet spread. It can be scooped directly from the jar onto toast and used to flavor ice cream, buttercream, or crème anglaise or other custards. An enriched version that includes milk, butter, and egg is a popular filling in Italy for flaky pastries like cannoncini, cream horns fashioned from puff pastry.

• Pistachio oil varies from golden to pale green and has an intense pistachio flavor. It can be used for light sautéing, but rarely is because of its high cost and its low smoke point of 250°F (120°C). In contrast, extra-virgin olive oil and butter have a smoke point of 350°F (175°C). It is best used as a finishing oil for vegetables, fish, and shellfish. It also makes an elegant vinaigrette, can be incorporated into dishes that traditionally use olive oil, such as hummus or pesto, or used in baking in cookies and cakes.

Homemade Pistachio Staples

While you can purchase pistachio milk, meal, flour, paste, and butter, you can also make them at home. Pistachio milk is made by soaking the raw kernels in water overnight, then processing them with fresh water in a high-speed blender or food processor and straining away the pulp. Pistachio meal, flour, paste, and butter are all made the same way. It is the degree of processing that creates the different results. Brief to moderate processing—just a minute or two—will produce coarse pistachio meal. Processing for a little bit longer— another minute or so—will yield finely ground flour. If you continue processing, you will end up with a slightly textured pistachio paste. Process for a bit longer and you will have a smooth butter.

Pistachio meal can be used in crumble toppings, pastry crusts, baked goods, and in lieu of bread crumbs. Pistachio flour can be substituted for all-purpose or whole-wheat flour, though it is often used in combination with them. Homemade pistachio paste and butter are 100 percent pistachios with no sweetener or other ingredients added unless you choose to add them.

Removing the Skin to Show Off the Green

Pistachio kernels vary in color from naturally bright green, slightly green, and pink tinged to yellowish. After shelling, they all have a brownish skin (seed coat). Removing the skin before processing will yield a more colorful end result. If the skin is left on, the pistachio products will be brownish or beige rather than greenish gold. However, the final color will be determined by the vibrancy of the green in the nuts themselves, which varies. The brown skin can be easily removed by blanching whole, shelled nuts in boiling water for 30 seconds, allowing them to dry fully, and then rubbing off the skins with a kitchen towel.

Pistachio Paste

Pistachio Butter

Pistachio Meal

Pistachio Flour

A Shell Worth Saving

You can amass quite a mound of shells while enjoying a handful of pistachio nuts. But before you compost or throw out that pile, consider a number of practical household solutions for them.

Pistachio shells are an ideal mulch component, mixed with wood chips, bark, leaves, or other organic material, for your garden beds. Over time, the shells slowly release nutrients to enrich your soil. Just make sure if you are using salted shells that you rinse them well first and let them dry. Too much salt is toxic to plants.

Use pistachio shells to line the bottom of potted plants. They'll prevent the plant from becoming waterlogged and aid drainage if the pot doesn't have a hole. The shells will eventually biodegrade.

Pesky garden critters can be kept at bay by spreading the shells in a thick layer around outdoor plants to prevent squirrels, and other interlopers from digging in the soil. You can use your salted shells to create a barricade against slugs and snails around individual plants or your garden perimeter.

And when you want to light a fire in a wood stove, pistachio shells make great kindling. If using the shells in an open fireplace or campfire, be sure to stand back after adding them. They contain oils that will cause them to pop and fly free of the fire ring.

—BLAKE HALLANAN, journalist

A Note about Pistachios in the Recipes

Unless otherwise specified, all the recipes in this book use unsalted, raw, shelled pistachios. Here is a quick reference showing US volume to metric equivalents for the various forms of pistachios used in the recipes, from whole nuts to flour. Note: If you have only salted pistachios on hand, you can substitute them for unsalted, adjusting the salt in the recipe to account for the additional salt.

1 cup whole pistachios = 140 grams
½ cup = 70 grams
⅓ cup = 45 grams
¼ cup = 35 grams

1 cup coarsely chopped = 120 grams
½ cup = 60 grams
⅓ cup = 40 grams
¼ cup = 30 grams

1 cup finely chopped = 100 grams
½ cup = 50 grams
⅓ cup = 35 grams
¼ cup = 25 grams

1 cup pistachio meal = 108 grams
½ cup = 54 grams
⅓ cup = 36 grams
¼ cup = 27 grams

1 cup pistachio flour = 112 grams
½ cup = 56 grams
⅓ cup = 37 grams
¼ cup = 28 grams

ABOVE: *In Turkey, the seeds from wild pistachio trees are roasted and ground to make a mock Turkish coffee.*

Pistachio Milk   Makes about 2 cups (480 ml)

1 cup (140 g) pistachios
½ teaspoon pure vanilla or almond extract (optional)
1 teaspoon agave nectar (optional)

In a bowl, combine the pistachios with 2 cups (480 ml) water. Let soak overnight at room temperature. The next day, drain the nuts and transfer them to a high-speed blender or a food processor and add 3 cups (720 ml) fresh water. Process until the nuts are finely ground and the mixture is milky.

Line a fine-mesh sieve with cheesecloth and set it over a bowl. Pour the pistachio mixture into the sieve and then press hard against the pulp with the back of a wooden spoon to release as much "milk" as possible. To add additional flavor and/or sweetness, stir in the vanilla and/or agave nectar. Transfer to an airtight container and refrigerate for up to 3 days.

Pistachio Meal and Flour   Makes 2 cups (216 g) meal and (224 g) flour

2 cups (280 g) pistachios

In a saucepan, bring 4 cups (960 ml) water to a boil over medium-high heat. Add the pistachios and boil for 30 seconds. Drain into a colander, then spread in a single layer on a sheet pan. Let stand overnight at room temperature until completely dry.

The next day, place the nuts on the center of a clean kitchen towel, fold the towel over the nuts, and rub the nuts with the towel to remove the brown skins. Not every bit of skin will come off, but enough will flake off to keep the meal a light green.

Transfer the skinned nuts to a food processor and process until the nuts are coarsely ground to your satisfaction for meal or until finely ground for flour. Store in an airtight container in the refrigerator for up to 1 month.

Pistachio Butter   Makes 1¾ cups (448 g)

2 cups (280 g) pistachios

In a saucepan, bring 4 cups (960 ml) water to a boil over medium-high heat. Add the pistachios and boil for 30 seconds. Drain into a colander, then spread in a single layer on a sheet pan. Let stand overnight at room temperature until completely dry.

The next day, place the nuts on the center of a clean kitchen towel, fold the towel over the nuts, and rub the nuts with the towel to remove the brown skins. Not every bit of skin will come off, but enough will flake off to keep the butter a light green.

Transfer the nuts to a food processor and process until creamy. Store in an airtight container in the refrigerator for up to 2 weeks.

Sweet Pistachio Paste   Makes ¾ cup (192 g)

½ cup (70 g) pistachios
⅔ cup (135 g) granulated sugar
⅓ to ½ cup (75 to 120 ml) whole milk

In a saucepan, bring 2 cups (480 ml) water to a boil over medium-high heat. Add the pistachios and boil for 30 seconds. Drain into a colander, then spread in a single layer on a sheet pan. Let stand overnight at room temperature until completely dry.

The next day, place the nuts on the center of a clean kitchen towel, fold the towel over the nuts, and rub the nuts with the towel to remove most of the brown skins.

Transfer the nuts to a food processor and process until the nuts are coarsely ground. Add the sugar and ⅓ cup (75 ml) of the milk and process until the nuts are more finely ground but not flour and the mixture is smooth, adding more of the milk as needed to achieve a good consistency. Store in an airtight container in the refrigerator for up to 1 week.

breakfasts & breads

pistachio flour waffles with pistachio butter and pomegranate syrup

Makes 3 to 4 four-square waffles; serves 4

Dominated by the characteristic nutty flavor and slightly grainy texture of pistachio flour, these unusual waffles take no longer to make than any other. Pistachio butter doubles the nut flavor, and the intense, jewel-like pomegranate syrup is mellowed with honey.

FOR THE SYRUP:

1 cup (240 ml) pomegranate syrup

½ cup (170 g) honey

1 teaspoon fresh lemon juice

FOR THE WAFFLES:

3 large eggs

1¼ cups (140 g) pistachio flour

1 cup (125 g) all-purpose flour

2 teaspoons baking powder

½ teaspoon fine sea salt

1½ cups (360 ml) whole milk

5½ tablespoons (75 g) unsalted butter, melted and cooled

1½ tablespoons sugar

Pistachio butter, for serving

⅓ cup (45 g) pistachios, coarsely chopped, for garnish

Preheat a four-square waffle iron. Preheat the oven to 225°F (110°C).

Make the syrup: In a small bowl, combine the pomegranate syrup and honey and mix well. Stir in the lemon juice. Transfer to a serving pitcher and set aside.

Make the waffles: Set two large bowls side by side. Separate each egg, allowing the whites to fall into one bowl and dropping the yolks into the second bowl. In a medium bowl, whisk together pistachio and all-purpose flours, the baking powder, and salt.

Pour the milk into the egg yolks and using an electric mixer, beat on medium speed until well blended. With the mixer running, slowly drizzle in the melted butter, beating until incorporated. Add the flour mixture and beat until smooth and creamy.

With clean beaters, beat the egg whites on high speed until stiff peaks form. Add the sugar in two batches, beating after each addition until once again stiff. Fold one-third of the egg whites into the flour–egg yolk mixture to lighten it, then gently fold in the remaining egg whites until no white streaks remain.

The waffle iron should now be hot. (If the plates of your waffle iron are not nonstick, brush them with melted butter or canola or other light cooking oil. Pour enough of the batter—about 1½ cups (360 ml)—onto the lower plate to cover it. Smooth it with a heat-resistant spatula if necessary. Close the lid and cook until steam is no longer visibly rising and the waffle is golden brown. This usually takes 2½ to 3 minutes. If your waffle iron has an indicator light, wait for it to signal the waffle is ready.

Gently remove the waffle from the iron, using a knife to lift the edges if needed. Transfer to a sheet pan and place in the oven to keep warm. Repeat until the batter is gone, two to three more times.

Serve immediately, topped with the pistachio butter and syrup and sprinkled with the pistachios.

breakfast bowl with black beans, poached egg, and pistachios   Serves 2

There's a good reason food bowls are so popular. One dish (the bowl) combines layers of ingredients with varying flavors, textures, and temperatures, all to be savored together, bite after bite. Here, beans plus an egg make a protein-rich base, pistachios add crunch and color, and spicy hot sauce keeps the temperature up. A drizzle of crema or a little pile of avocado cubes would be good too. And maybe some cilantro? The possibilities are endless.

If the beans are canned, drain and rinse them. In a saucepan, combine the beans, olive oil, and fine sea salt and warm over medium-high heat, stirring often, until hot, 3 to 4 minutes. Remove from the heat.

Divide the beans between two individual bowls and top each bowl with an egg. Divide the cherry tomatoes, avocado, and pickled onion evenly between the bowls. Add a large spoonful of salsa to each bowl, then sprinkle with the cilantro, flaky sea salt, and pepper. Finish with the pistachios, dividing them evenly, and a drizzle of pistachio oil. Serve immediately.

2 cups (340 g) drained, cooked homemade or canned black beans

2 teaspoons extra-virgin olive oil

½ teaspoon fine sea salt

2 large eggs, poached or fried

12 cherry tomatoes, halved

1 avocado, pitted, peeled, and diced

Pickled red onion, for topping

¼ cup (45 g) store-bought or homemade salsa

Small handful cilantro leaves

Flaky sea salt, such as Maldon, and freshly ground black pepper

⅓ cup (45 g) pistachios, coarsely chopped

Pistachio oil, for drizzling

strawberry and pistachio yogurt parfait   Serves 1

One of the great things about pistachios is that the pretty green nut adds color and charm to just about any dish. It's perfect to use in a vibrant, show-offy yogurt parfait, where the layers of fruit and nuts shine through the glass. Depending on what's in season, change out the strawberries for nectarines, plums, blueberries, or even oranges. The good news is that pistachios go equally well with whatever fruit you choose. You can also use regular yogurt instead of Greek style.

Spoon half of the yogurt into a serving glass. Top with half of the berries and then half of the pistachios. Repeat the layers, ending with a layer of pistachios. Serve immediately.

1 cup (200 g) plain Greek yogurt (whole milk, low-fat, or nonfat)

1½ cups (215 g) strawberries, hulled and sliced

⅓ cup (45 g) pistachios, coarsely chopped

savory onion and pistachio strata with fresh herbs Serves 4

With ingredients and style that work for both breakfast and lunch, moist and creamy stratas, the eggier cousins of bread pudding, are poster children for brunch time. This one is vegetarian, focusing on onions and pistachios, but sausage could be added for the omnivores. Sliced tomatoes are all you need on the side, but a little kimchi is a good idea too.

12 to 14 slices day-old baguette

2 cups (480 ml) whole milk

3 tablespoons unsalted butter

4 medium yellow onions, thinly sliced (about 4 cups/460 g)

5 large eggs

1 teaspoon fine sea salt

½ teaspoon freshly ground black pepper

½ cup (60 g) grated Parmesan cheese

8 ounces (225 g) Gruyère or Emmental cheese, slivered

½ cup (20 g) chopped mixed fresh herbs, such as flat-leaf parsley, chives, and oregano

⅓ cup (45 g) whole pistachios, plus ½ cup (60 g) coarsely chopped

Preheat the oven to 350°F (175°C).

Put the bread into a large bowl and pour in the milk, covering the slices completely. Let stand until the bread is soft, about 5 minutes, or more if the bread is quite dry. Remove the bread, lightly squeezing each slice to release the excess milk back into the bowl. Set the bread and the milk aside.

In a frying pan, melt the 2 tablespoons of the butter over medium-high heat. Add the onions and stir to coat with the butter. Reduce the heat to low and cook, stirring from time to time, until the onions are soft and lightly golden, 10 to 12 minutes. Remove from the heat.

In a bowl, whisk together the eggs, salt, pepper, and ½ cup (120 ml) of the reserved milk.

Grease an 8-inch (20-cm) square baking dish with the remaining 1 tablespoon butter. Layer half of the bread slices in the bottom of the dish. Top with half of the cooked onions, half of the Parmesan, and half of the Gruyère. Sprinkle with half of the herb mixture and half of the whole pistachios. Repeat the layers. Pour the egg mixture over the layers, letting it seep down the sides.

Bake the strata until the top is golden brown and a toothpick inserted into the center comes out clean, about 40 minutes.

Remove from the oven and scatter the chopped pistachios evenly over the top. Let rest for 10 minutes, then cut into 4-inch (10-cm) squares and serve.

baked eggs with pistachios, harissa, and mint   Serves 4

This is a classic French dish with a contemporary twist. North African harissa, a heady, chile-based, paste, flavors the tomato mixture; aromatic, fresh mint leaves line and garnish each ramekin, and a topping of chopped pistachios adds a rich, crunchy finish. Serve with buttered toast fingers for dipping into the spicy tomato mixture and runny yolk.

Preheat the oven to 425°F (220°C).

In a frying pan, heat the oil over medium-high heat. When the oil is hot, add the onion and cook, stirring frequently, until soft, about 3 minutes. Add the tomatoes, salt, and pepper and cook, stirring, until the tomatoes begin to release their juices, about 2 minutes. Reduce the heat to medium and continue to cook, stirring occasionally, until the juices are absorbed and the mixture has thickened, 3 to 4 minutes. Stir in the harissa to taste and remove from the heat.

Divide half of the mint leaves evenly among four ½-cup (120-ml) ramekins, arranging them on the bottoms. Pour about ¼ cup (60 ml) of the tomato mixture into each ramekin. (You may have more than you need; reserve the remainder for another use. Crack an egg into each ramekin. Cover each ramekin snugly with aluminum foil and place in a baking dish large enough to hold them without touching. Pour water into the baking dish to reach halfway up the sides of the ramekins.

Carefully place the baking dish in the oven. Bake until the whites of the eggs are just set and the yolks are still slightly runny (or until done to your liking), 8 to 10 minutes. To check, lift the foil on a ramekin or two.

Remove from the oven, remove the foil, and sprinkle each with the remaining mint and pistachios. Serve hot.

1 tablespoon extra-virgin olive oil

¼ cup (45 g) minced yellow onion

4 medium tomatoes, chopped

½ teaspoon fine sea salt

¼ teaspoon freshly ground black pepper

1 to 2 teaspoons harissa

¼ cup (20 g) small fresh mint leaves, chopped if large

4 large eggs

⅓ cup (45 g) pistachios, coarsely chopped

avocado toast with microgreens, pistachios, and parmesan   Serves 2

The true origins of avocado toast may never be ascertained, but the now-ubiquitous breakfast favorite appears to have started in Australia in 1993 when a Sydney chef put it on his menu. However, Southern Californians who grew up in the 1950s can attest to it being a part of their food world long before its global popularity. Today, the toast has gone well beyond the basic crushed avocado, salt, and pepper to just about anything a cook fancies. Pistachios, for one, make an excellent topping: colorful, flavorful, and crunchy. Some salty cheese and a sprinkle of microgreens are added here, but the only real limit is the creator's imagination.

Toast the bread slices in a toaster or toaster oven, then place each slice on a plate.

With a sharp knife, cut the avocado in half. Carefully remove the pit, prying it away with the tip of the knife. With each avocado half still in its skin, cut it lengthwise into slices ½ inch (12 mm) thick, being careful not to pierce the skin.

Slide the knife between the flesh and the skin of an avocado half to remove the slices and arrange slices on a piece of toast. Repeat with the remaining avocado half, topping the second piece of toast.

Sprinkle the avocado with the salt and pepper, followed by the microgreens and pistachios. Top with the cheese and serve.

Variations
- Mashed avocado, pomegranate arils (seeds), crumbled feta cheese, chopped pistachios
- Mashed avocado, smoked salmon slices, capers, goat cheese, fresh dill sprigs, chopped pistachios
- Cubed avocado, chopped hard-cooked egg, bay shrimp, radish slices, chopped pistachios
- Cubed avocado, cherry tomato halves, crisp bacon crumbles or slices, fresh marjoram leaves, chopped pistachios
- Sliced avocado, tomato slices, burrata cheese, fresh basil leaves, chopped pistachios

2 slices whole-grain bread

1 avocado

¼ teaspoon fine sea salt

¼ teaspoon freshly ground black pepper

½ cup (15 g) microgreens

⅓ cup (45 g) pistachios, coarsely chopped

½ cup (55 g) shaved Parmesan cheese

sausage and pistachio flatbread with arugula
Makes about 12 pieces; serves 4

Technically speaking, this is a pizza because it is made with a yeast dough. But the topping is light and has no tomato, making it more akin to a flatbread, which is traditionally made without yeast and is rarely spread with tomato sauce or substantial toppings. Covered with a salad-like mixture of arugula and feta under which nuts and sausage are hidden. Serve this for any meal—breakfast, lunch, or dinner.

FOR THE DOUGH:

1 package (2¼ teaspoons) active dry yeast

1 cup (240 ml) lukewarm water (105° to 115°F/40° to 46°C)

½ teaspoon sugar

1 teaspoon fine sea salt

3 tablespoons extra-virgin olive oil

2¾ to 3 cups (345 to 375 g) all-purpose flour, plus more for dusting

FOR THE TOPPING:

12 ounces (340 g) mild Italian sausage, casings removed

2 teaspoons dried oregano

3 ounces (85 g) feta cheese, crumbled (about ½ cup)

2 tablespoons extra-virgin olive oil

½ cup (60 g) coarsely chopped pistachios

1 cup (20 g) arugula leaves

Make the dough: In a small bowl, dissolve the yeast in the water and then stir in the sugar. Let stand until foamy, about 5 minutes.

Pour the yeast mixture into a food processor and add the salt, 2 tablespoons of the oil, and 2 cups (250 g) of the flour. Pulse while gradually adding more flour until the dough comes together in a soft ball. The dough should be neither too dry nor too sticky and should not stick to your fingers.

Turn the dough out onto a lightly floured work surface and knead until smooth and elastic, about 7 minutes. Shape into a ball.

Oil a large bowl with the remaining 1 tablespoon oil. Add the dough ball to the bowl and then turn the ball to coat on all sides with oil. Cover the bowl with a damp kitchen towel and leave the dough to rise in a warm, draft-free area until doubled in size, 1½ to 2 hours.

While the dough is rising, begin preparing the topping: Heat a frying pan over medium-high heat, add the sausage, and cook, stirring often and breaking up the meat with a wooden spoon or spatula, just until pink, about 5 minutes. Using a slotted utensil, transfer to a plate and set aside.

Place a pizza stone or sturdy sheet pan in the oven and preheat the oven to 500°F (260°C).

When the dough is ready, lightly flour the work surface. Punch down the dough and turn it out onto the floured surface. With a rolling pin, start rolling from the center outward, rotating the dough as needed and flipping it over once, until you have an oval about 15 inches (40 cm) long, 12 inches (30.5 cm) wide, and ¼ inch (6 mm) thick. Lightly dust a pizza peel or cookie sheet with a little flour. Transfer the rolled-out dough onto the floured peel or pan.

Brush the entire surface of the dough, including the edge, with some of the oil, coating it lightly. Sprinkle evenly with the sausage, half of the oregano, and half of the feta.

Carefully transfer the flatbread to the pizza stone or sheet pan and bake until the crust is puffed and golden along the edge and the bottom is crisp and golden, about 15 minutes.

Remove from the oven and immediately brush the edge of the crust with more oil. Sprinkle evenly with the remaining feta and oregano followed by all the pistachios and arugula. Cut into irregular squares and triangles to serve.

A Gift from the Ottomans

Long common throughout the Middle East, pistachios are relative newcomers to parts of North Africa, where I was born. In Morocco, almonds or walnuts have been part of the agricultural and culinary heritage for centuries. Not so for pistachios, which have only been planted since the 1980s and are beyond the reach of most households.

The same holds true in Algeria. "Pistachios are an expensive ingredient, though Algerian cooks are beginning to use them in traditional pastries for celebrations such as weddings or the first day of Ramadan," says Nacira Winner, an Algerian friend who enjoys preparing the foods of her native country. They are mainly used in eastern Algeria, closer to the Tunisian border. Algeria's pistachio crops are increasing yearly, as they are in Morocco, because the drought-tolerant trees adapt well to the countries' higher elevations.

Unlike their neighbors, Tunisian cooks have long made use of pistachios in baklava, kafteji (fried vegetables), and rice pilaf. They owe this predilection to the Ottomans, who invaded Tunisia at the end of the sixteenth century and introduced their newly conquered territories to dishes that included pistachios. North African cuisine has long adopted influences from around the Mediterranean basin. No doubt, pistachios will one day join the ranks of such "traditional" ingredients.

—KITTY MORSE, author of ten cookbooks,
including *Cooking at the Kasbah:
Recipes from My Moroccan Kitchen*

orange and pistachio scones   Makes 12 scones

Fragrant with the scent of oranges, these light, flaky scones, richly dotted with chunky pistachios, make festive fare for your breakfast or teatime crowd. Drizzle or slather them with the orange-infused icing, depending on how much sweetness your guests prefer.

FOR THE SCONES:

2⅓ cups (290 g) all-purpose flour, plus more for dusting

¼ cup (50 g) granulated sugar

2 teaspoons baking powder

½ teaspoon baking soda

¼ teaspoon fine sea salt

½ cup (115 g) cold unsalted butter, cut into pieces

¾ cup (170 g) whole-milk plain yogurt

1 large egg

¾ cup (105 g) pistachios, coarsely chopped

Freshly grated zest of 1 orange

FOR THE ICING:

1½ cups (180 g) confectioners' sugar

1 orange

½ teaspoon orange blossom water

Preheat the oven to 350°F (175°C). Line a sheet pan with parchment paper or a silicone baking mat.

Make the scones: In a food processor, combine the flour, granulated sugar, baking powder, baking soda, and salt and pulse three or four times to mix. Add the butter and pulse until the butter is incorporated and the mixture looks a little crumbly, about 1 minute. Set aside.

In a bowl, whisk together the yogurt and egg until blended. Add the pistachios and the orange zest; whisk to mix. Pour the yogurt-egg mixture into the food processor and process just until the flour is incorporated and the dough clumps together, 3 to 4 seconds. Do not overprocess. The dough will be sticky and wet.

Lightly flour a work surface. Scrape the dough onto the floured surface and lightly sprinkle the dough with a little flour. Fold the dough over onto itself and push down, then repeat two or three times. Divide the dough in half. With a rolling pin, roll out each half into a disk about ½ inch (12 mm) thick. With a sharp knife, cut each disk into 6 wedges.

Transfer the wedges to the prepared sheet pan, spacing them about 1 inch (2.5 cm) apart. Bake the scones until they are lightly browned, about 18 minutes.

While the scones are baking, make the icing: Put the confectioners' sugar into a bowl. Grate 2 tablespoons orange zest and squeeze 2 tablespoons of orange juice. Add the zest, juice, and the orange blossom water to the sugar and mix well with a wooden spoon or whisk. The icing should be somewhat stiff. If it is too runny, mix in more sugar. If too stiff, add a tiny bit more orange juice.

When the scones are ready, transfer them to a wire rack set over a sheet pan. While they are still warm, drizzle them with the icing, then let set for a few minutes. Serve the scones warm or at room temperature. Store any leftover scones in an airtight container at room temperature for up to 4 days.

starters & snacks

cumin-roasted cocktail pistachios

Makes 2 cups (227 g); serves 4

Part of the fun of eating pistachios is breaking them out of their shells. This addictive spice mix is the perfect coating for a pistachio snack, and although you can use shelled pistachios, in-shell nuts are more visually appealing and more fun to eat while sipping your favorite cocktail. Although any leftover nuts can be stored in the refrigerator, they'll probably be devoured in one sitting!

1 tablespoon extra-virgin olive oil

1 tablespoon ground cumin

1½ teaspoons fine sea salt

2 cups (227 g) raw, in-shell pistachios

2 teaspoons Aleppo pepper
   (see Note) or freshly ground
   black pepper

Line a platter or sheet pan with paper towels and set it near the stove.

In a frying pan large enough to hold the pistachios in a single layer, heat the oil over medium-high heat. Stir in the cumin and salt. Add the pistachios and cook, turning from time to time to prevent burning, until the nuts are fragrant and lightly browned, about 5 minutes. Stir in the pepper and remove from the heat.

Using a slotted spoon or spatula, lift the pistachios to the towel-lined platter. Using a spoon, scoop up any spices left behind and sprinkle over the pistachios. Let stand at room temperature for several hours until dry.

Scoop the pistachios into a serving bowl and serve. They will keep in an airtight container at room temperature for up to 3 days or in the refrigerator for up to 3 weeks.

Note: Mildly spicy Aleppo pepper originated in Syria and is now grown in Turkey as well. It is sold dried and crushed or ground (either will work here) in groceries specializing in Middle Eastern foods, in well-stocked supermarkets, and online.

toasted pistachios, cashews, almonds, and dried olive snack mix

Serves 3 or 4

Herbs and chili powder spice up this medley of pistachios, almonds, and cashews, used in equal measure, but the salty tang of this snack mix comes from the Mediterranean-style oil-cured olives. The mix can be prepared up to several days in advance and kept refrigerated, which makes it an easy snack to pull out when friends drop by for drinks.

Preheat the oven to 350°F (175°C).

In a baking pan large enough to hold all the nuts and olives in a single layer, combine the almonds, cashews, pistachios, olives, oil, herbes de Provence, and chili powder and mix well. Spread the nuts in a single layer.

Toast the snack mix for 5 minutes, then stir well and spread in a single layer again. Continue to toast the snack mix until fragrant and nuts are slightly browned, about 6 minutes longer.

Remove from the oven and let cool completely in the pan, about 1 hour. Using a slotted spoon, transfer the snack mix to a serving bowl, leaving any excess oil behind. Add the salt and toss well.

Serve the snack mix at room temperature. It will keep in an airtight container in the refrigerator for up to 10 days or in the freezer for up to 6 months.

1 cup (140 g) whole raw almonds

1 cup (120 g) whole raw cashews

1 cup (140 g) pistachios

⅓ cup (45 g) pitted oil-cured black olives

1 tablespoon extra-virgin olive oil

1 teaspoon herbes de Provence

½ teaspoon chili powder

1 teaspoon coarse sea salt

goat cheese log with pistachio pesto

Serves 4 to 6

1 log (4 ounces/115 g) fresh goat cheese

3 tablespoons Pistachio Pesto (recipe follows)

Pistachio oil, for drizzling

2 tablespoons coarsely chopped toasted pistachios

Pistachio pesto, a California take on the Italian favorite, is as versatile as its traditional Mediterranean cousin and can be used on everything from pasta to vegetables. Here it's used to dress up goat cheese to serve as an appetizer with baguette toasts, crackers, or a selection of crudités. When your platter is assembled, drizzle the goat cheese with a little pistachio oil to accentuate the pistachio flavor of the tasty pesto.

Place the cheese log on a small platter or plate and top with the pesto. Drizzle with a little pistachio oil, sprinkle with the pistachios, and serve.

pistachio pesto   Makes about 1 cup (240 g)

2½ cups (75 g) packed fresh basil leaves

⅓ cup (70 g) pistachios

½ cup (50 g) grated Parmesan cheese

¼ teaspoon freshly ground black pepper

½ to 1 teaspoon fine sea salt

⅓ cup (60 ml) extra-virgin olive oil

1 tablespoon pistachio oil

In a food processor, combine the basil, pistachios, cheese, pepper, and salt and process until coarsely ground. With the processor running, slowly drizzle in the olive and pistachio oils, continuing to process until smooth.

To store the pesto, spoon into a jar or other container, top with a thin film of olive oil to prevent discoloring, cap tightly, and refrigerate for up to 5 days or freeze for up to 6 months.

pistachio-fennel crackers   Makes 24 crackers

Get your hors d'oeuvre platter ready! These easy-to-make crackers have so much flavor you'll want to enjoy them on their own, but they also shine with cheese and dips. Baked to crispy perfection, they pair well with Pistachio Cheese Spread with Roasted Poblanos and Garlic (page 80) and Hummus with Pistachio Oil and Fresh Herbs with Crudités (page 76).

Preheat the oven to 350°F (175°C). Line a sheet pan with parchment paper.

In a mortar with a pestle or in a small bowl with a wooden spoon, crush 1½ teaspoons of the fennel seeds. In a medium bowl, combine the flour, baking powder, pistachios, salt, pepper, the crushed fennel, and the remaining ½ teaspoon whole fennel seeds. Whisk to blend well.

Make a well in the center of the flour mixture and pour the egg, 3½ tablespoons water, and the oil into the well. Then, using a wooden spoon, gradually draw the flour mixture into the liquid and stir until the dry ingredients are evenly moistened and come together in a soft but not sticky ball. Wrap the dough in plastic wrap and refrigerate for 30 minutes.

On a lightly floured work surface, roll out the dough into a rectangle ⅛ inch (3 mm) thick or thinner. Using a sharp knife or fluted pastry or pasta cutter, cut the dough lengthwise into strips 1 inch (2.5 cm) wide. Then cut crosswise into equal rectangles about 2 inches (5 cm) long.

Transfer the crackers to the prepared sheet pan, spacing them about ½ inch (12 mm) apart. Prick each cracker twice with the tines of a fork.

Bake the crackers until lightly golden, 10 to 12 minutes. Turn off the oven heat and let the crackers cool in the oven with the oven door ajar for 30 minutes. Remove from the oven, transfer to wire racks, and let cool completely before serving. The crackers will keep in an airtight container at room temperature for up to 5 days.

2 teaspoons fennel seeds

1¼ cups (155 g) all-purpose flour, plus more for dusting

¼ teaspoon baking powder

¼ cup (25 g) finely chopped pistachios

1 teaspoon fine sea salt

¼ teaspoon freshly ground black pepper

1 large egg, lightly beaten

3½ tablespoons extra-virgin olive oil

hummus with pistachio oil and fresh herbs with crudités

Makes about 2 cups (450 g)

¾ cup (150 g) dry chickpeas, picked over and rinsed, or 1 can (15 ounces/430 g) chickpeas

⅓ cup (80 ml) fresh lemon juice (about 2 lemons)

2 tablespoons tahini (sesame seed paste)

3 tablespoons pistachio oil

2 cloves garlic, finely minced

1 teaspoon fine sea salt

1 tablespoon mixed chopped fresh chives and flat-leaf parsley

Vegetable crudités, such as celery, carrot, and jicama sticks; thinly sliced radishes; broccoli and cauliflower florets; blanched green beans; and/or bell pepper strips, for serving

This popular Middle Eastern table staple is typically made with olive oil, but using pistachio oil in its place nicely plays off the nutty, sweet flavor of the chickpeas. Although pita or other flatbreads are the usual accompaniment, an assortment of vegetable crudités is equally good for scooping up the creamy dip.

If using dry chickpeas, in a saucepan, combine the chickpeas with water to cover by 3 inches (7.5 cm) and bring to a boil over medium-high heat. Reduce the heat to a simmer and cook, uncovered, until tender, 1½ to 2 hours, adding more water if needed to keep the chickpeas covered. Drain the chickpeas into a sieve placed over a bowl to capture the cooking liquid. Let cool.

If using canned chickpeas, drain them into a colander placed in the sink, then rinse under cold running water and drain well.

In a blender or food processor, combine the home-cooked or canned chickpeas, lemon juice, tahini, 2 tablespoons of the oil, garlic, and salt and process until smooth, adding 2 to 3 tablespoons of the chickpea cooking liquid or water as needed to achieve a creamy paste.

Spoon the hummus into a small serving bowl, drizzle with the remaining 1 tablespoon oil, and sprinkle with the herbs. Serve with the crudités. The hummus will keep in an airtight container in the refrigerator for up to 1 week.

pistachio-olive tapenade

Makes about 2½ cups (560 g)

2 cups (225 g) pitted green olives

1 cup (140 g) whole pistachios, plus 1 tablespoon coarsely chopped for garnish

1 teaspoon minced fresh thyme

2 olive oil-packed anchovy fillets

2 teaspoons drained capers

2 teaspoons fresh lemon juice

2 tablespoons pistachio oil

1 tablespoon extra-virgin olive oil

The soft pale green that emerges from combining briny green olives with pistachios makes an eye-catching spread that is amenable to bright garnishes, such as pink peppercorns, prosciutto, or pomegranate seeds. Rich and complex, the spread is also a complementary topping for grilled fish or roasted vegetables.

In a food processor, combine the olives, whole pistachios, thyme, anchovies, capers, and lemon juice and process until the pistachios and olives are ground. Add the pistachio oil and olive oil and process until a smooth paste forms. If the mixture is too thick, add a little more olive oil until you have a good consistency.

Spoon into a small serving bowl, garnish with the chopped pistachios, and serve immediately. The tapenade will keep in an airtight container in the refrigerator for up to 5 days.

Global Pistachio Celebrations

It seems appropriate that a nut with such a rich and international history has annual festivals in its honor around the world. In the United States, National Pistachio Day is celebrated each year on February 26, and pistachio lovers are encouraged to take selfies while eating pistachios to share on social media with the hashtag #PistachioDay.

Sicily hosts its yearly pistachio festivals the second Sunday of October in Catania and in mid- to late September in Agrigento. Festivalgoers rejoice as they sample their favorite nut in pastas, arancini, and confections. The festival also includes side events and conferences about the celebrated nut.

In Greece, the popular Fistiki Fest is held on the island of Aegina at the end of each harvesting season, in September. The festival welcomes large crowds of pistachio enthusiasts who come to attend a full program of events and sample the popular nut in a variety of local products, from liqueurs to nut butters to ice creams.

Iran hosts an annual pistachio celebration in the ancient city of Damghan, which is famous for its pistachio orchards. Farmers and growers attend this scientific, cultural, and economic event, and can witness traditional pistachio harvesting and buy nuts fresh from local farms.

Every fall, Gaziantep, Turkey, which UNESCO has named a Creative City of Gastronomy, holds a three-day Gaziantep Pistachio Culture and Art Festival. The event celebrates not only the native pistachios, the city's world-renowned pistachio baklava, and the diverse local cuisine but also the music, art, and literature of the region.

—BLAKE HALLANAN, journalist

crostini with white beans, sautéed greens, and toasted pistachios

Makes 12 crostini; serves 4 to 6

Italian crostini are a host's best friend: they're easy to make and can be topped with just about anything delicious to create an instant appetizer. Inspired by the Tuscan combination of white beans and greens, these bite-size crostini are warm and hearty and can also be served as a first course. Finishing with a sprinkle of toasted pistachios and a drizzle of pistachio oil elevates them a notch. Spinach is used here, but other greens, such as sautéed broccoli rabe, kale, or chard, can be substituted.

Make the beans: In a saucepan, melt the butter over medium heat. When it foams, add the onion and cook, stirring frequently, until translucent, about 2 minutes.

If using dry beans, add them to the pan and stir for a few minutes. Then pour in water to cover the beans by 3 inches (7.5 cm), raise the heat to medium-high, and bring to a boil. Reduce the heat to low, cover, and cook for 30 minutes. Add the salt and pepper, re-cover, and continue to cook until the beans are tender to the bite, about 1 hour longer. Taste for seasoning and adjust with salt and pepper if needed. Drain into a fine-mesh sieve placed over a bowl to capture the cooking liquid. Measure 1½ cups (270 g) of the cooked beans into a bowl and add ½ cup (120 ml) of the cooking liquid to the beans. Reserve the remainder of the beans for another use.

If using canned beans, add them to the butter and onion along with ½ cup (120 ml) water. Bring to a simmer over medium heat and cook gently, stirring occasionally, for 10 minutes. Season with the salt and pepper, then taste and adjust the seasoning if needed. Transfer the beans and their liquid to a bowl.

Using a wooden spoon, crush some of the beans, leaving others whole. Cover to keep warm and set aside.

Rinse the spinach and transfer to a colander. In a frying pan, melt the butter over medium heat. When it foams, add the spinach, garlic, salt, and pepper and sauté until the spinach is limp but still bright green, about 1 minute.

To serve, spoon some of the warm beans onto each toasted baguette slice, top with some spinach and then a sprinkle of pistachios. Drizzle with a little oil and serve.

FOR THE BEANS:

4 tablespoons (55 g) unsalted butter

½ yellow onion, minced

1 cup (200 g) dry small white beans, such as Great Northern or cannellini, picked over and rinsed, or 1 can (15 ounces/430 g) small white beans, rinsed and drained

1 teaspoon fine sea salt

½ teaspoon freshly ground black pepper

4 cups (120 g) baby spinach

1 tablespoon unsalted butter

2 cloves garlic, minced

1 teaspoon fine sea salt

½ teaspoon freshly ground black pepper

12 slices baguette, toasted

⅓ cup (40 g) coarsely chopped toasted pistachios

Pistachio oil, for drizzling

pistachio cheese spread with roasted poblanos and garlic

Makes about 2½ cups (480 g)

Reminiscent of pimento cheese, this cheese spread calls for the large, deep green poblano chile favored by cooks in the Southwest and Mexico and includes chunky pistachio bits for crunch and color. Perfect for crackers or baguette toasts, the spread can also be tucked into grilled cheese sandwiches, where it gives each bite just enough heat to spice up lunchtime. It also makes a delicious stuffing for baked potatoes or an easy filling for that perennial party favorite, celery sticks.

1 large poblano chile

2½ cups (280 g) grated white Cheddar cheese (10 ounces)

2 tablespoons mayonnaise, plus more if needed

2 tablespoons pistachio meal

1 teaspoon poblano chile powder

½ clove garlic, minced

½ teaspoon white pepper

½ teaspoon fine sea salt

⅓ cup (45 g) pistachios, chopped

To roast the chile, preheat the broiler. Set the chile on a small sheet pan and broil about 6 inches (15 cm) from the heat source, turning as needed, until the skin is blistered and charred on all sides, 10 to 15 minutes. Alternatively, preheat a stovetop grill pan and roast the chile, turning as needed, until the skin is blistered and charred on all sides, about 5 minutes per side. Set the chile aside to cool. Peel away the charred skin and discard, using a paper towel to remove any clinging bits. Slit the chile lengthwise and remove and discard the stem and seeds. Coarsely chop the flesh.

In a bowl, using a wooden spoon, mix together the cheese and mayonnaise until well blended. Add the pistachio meal, chile powder, garlic, white pepper, salt, chopped chile, and all but 2 tablespoons of the pistachios and mix well. If the spread is too stiff, mix in a little more mayonnaise.

Spoon into a serving dish, garnish with the remaining pistachios, and serve. The spread will keep in an airtight container in the refrigerator for up to 1 week.

grilled halloumi with pistachio-garlic toasts   Serves 3 or 4

A traditional Cypriot cheese, halloumi has a firm texture and high melting point, which makes it one of the few cheeses that can be grilled or fried. It has an almost feta-like flavor but is slightly sweeter. Here, it is served hot off the grill with crunchy, garlicky toasts and a side salad of cherry tomatoes, cucumber, and red onion—a combination that makes a good beginning to nearly any meal. If you like, increase the quantities, and you'll have a main course.

In a bowl, combine the tomatoes, onion, and cucumber. Sprinkle with the salt, add the olive oil and oregano, and turn several times. Set aside.

Prepare a charcoal or gas grill for cooking over medium-high heat, or preheat a stovetop grill pan over medium-high heat.

When the grill or grill pan is ready, brush both sides of each baguette slice with some of the pistachio oil and grill, turning once, until lightly golden on both sides, about 1 minute per side.

Transfer the toasts to a plate. Using the garlic cloves, rub one side of each toast with garlic and then brush a little more pistachio oil on the garlic-rubbed side. Sprinkle the toasts with the pistachio meal, dividing it evenly. Set aside.

Place the halloumi slices on the grill or grill pan and cook just until grill marks form on the underside, about 2 minutes. Turn and grill until the second side has grill marks, about 1 minute longer. The slices should be crusty on the outside and soft and creamy on the inside.

Transfer the hot cheese to individual plates or a platter. Serve immediately accompanied by the toasts and the tomato salad.

2 cups (340 g) cherry tomatoes, halved

¼ red onion, finely chopped

½ large cucumber, finely chopped

½ teaspoon fine sea salt

2 tablespoons extra-virgin olive oil

1 tablespoon fresh oregano leaves

12 slices baguette

¼ cup (60 ml) pistachio oil

2 cloves garlic, peeled

½ cup (54 g) pistachio meal

8 ounces (225 g) halloumi cheese, sliced ¾ inch (2 cm) thick

grilled zucchini skewers with pistachio dukkah

Makes 12 skewers; serves 4

FOR THE DUKKAH:

1 tablespoon fennel seeds

1 tablespoon cumin seeds

2½ teaspoons coriander seeds

2 teaspoons sesame seeds

1 teaspoon nigella seeds

½ teaspoon black peppercorns

2 cups (280 g) pistachios

1 teaspoon Spanish smoked paprika

¾ teaspoon fine sea salt

FOR THE ZUCCHINI SKEWERS:

2 medium green zucchini
(8 to 10 ounces/225 to 280 g each)

2 medium yellow zucchini
(8 to 10 ounces/225 to 280 g each)

3 tablespoons extra-virgin olive oil

½ teaspoon fine sea salt

Finishing skewered zucchini ribbons with an abundant sprinkling of dukkah, the captivating Middle Eastern nut and spice mixture, is a change from the more traditional seasoning of thyme or oregano. Israeli-born Ben Poremba, the chef and restaurateur behind Bengelina Hospitality Group, headquartered in Saint Louis, contributed this pistachio dukkah recipe, which is nutty, spicy, and bright. Use the dukkah anytime you want to add an intriguing flavor. For example, sprinkle a little on avocado toast (see page 57), atop a bowl of hummus (see page 76), or on a simple green salad.

Make the dukkah: One at a time, toast the fennel, cumin, coriander, sesame, and nigella seeds on the stovetop. Put the seeds into a small, dry frying pan over medium-high heat. Toast, shaking the pan frequently to prevent burning, until the seeds deepen slightly in color and are fragrant. Pour into a small bowl to cool. The fennel, cumin, sesame, and nigella seeds will take about 2 minutes. The coriander seeds will take up to 5 minutes.

In a food processor, combine the cooled seeds, the peppercorns, and pistachios and pulse until finely ground, about 2 minutes. Transfer to a bowl, add the paprika and salt, and mix well. You will have more dukkah than you need for this recipe. The remainder will keep in an airtight container in a cool, dark cupboard for up to 2 weeks.

Make the zucchini skewers: Have ready twelve wooden skewers. Using a vegetable peeler or mandoline, cut each zucchini into lengthwise slices a scant ⅛ inch (3 mm) thick. If the slices are too thick, they will break when threading.

Thread each skewer with slices of the green and yellow zucchini, alternating the colors and folding each slice accordion-style. Line up the loaded skewers on a sheet pan, then drizzle with the oil and sprinkle with the salt.

Prepare a charcoal or gas grill for cooking over medium-high heat, or preheat a stovetop grill pan over medium-high heat.

When the grill or grill pan is ready, add the zucchini skewers and grill until slightly golden on the underside, about 2 minutes. Then turn and grill on the second side until slightly golden, about 1 minute longer.

Transfer to a platter, dust generously with the dukkah, and serve.

salads & sides

nectarine and burrata salad with chopped pistachio vinaigrette Serves 4

Warm weather brings juicy stone fruit, which is the perfect partner for creamy Italian burrata. The combination makes a delightful first course for an alfresco meal, though it is so delicious it could almost be a dessert. Dressed with an unusual chopped pistachio vinaigrette that's enlivened with balsamic vinegar and pistachio oil, this sweet and savory dish will be your new go-to summer salad.

FOR THE VINAIGRETTE:

⅓ cup (45 g) pistachios, toasted and coarsely chopped

¼ cup (60 ml) white balsamic vinegar

2 teaspoons pistachio oil

¼ teaspoon fine sea salt

5 ripe nectarines, halved, pitted, and cut into wedges 1 inch (2.5 cm) thick

4 ounces (115 g) burrata cheese, divided into 4 equal portions

¼ cup (20 g) fresh mint leaves, preferably small

¼ teaspoon New Mexico, ancho, or other chile powder or sweet paprika

Make the vinaigrette: Set aside 1 tablespoon of the pistachios for garnish. In a small bowl, using a fork, stir together the remaining pistachios, the vinegar, oil, and salt.

Divide the nectarine wedges evenly among four salad plates, arranging them in an attractive pile. Top each pile with a portion of burrata. Drizzle the salads with the vinaigrette, dividing it evenly. Garnish with the reserved pistachios and the mint leaves, sprinkle with the chile powder, and serve.

tabbouleh with pistachios and golden raisins Serves 4

Cool and refreshing, with spritely flavors of lemon and mint, this versatile salad is equally at home on a picnic buffet and an elegant dinner table. Serve the tabbouleh atop lettuce leaves or arrange the leaves around the salad for scooping.

In a small bowl, combine the bulgur and water, cover, and let stand for 20 minutes. Drain into a fine-mesh sieve lined with cheesecloth and press against the bulgur with the back of spoon to release all the water.

Transfer the bulgur to a bowl, add the parsley, mint, green onions, lemon juice, oil, and salt and mix well. Add the raisins and most of the pistachios and gently mix again.

To serve, spoon the tabbouleh into a serving bowl or onto a platter and surround with the lettuce leaves, or line four salad plates with the leaves and spoon the tabbouleh on top.

⅓ cup (45 g) medium-grind bulgur wheat

¼ cup (60 ml) warm water

3 cups (180 g) chopped fresh flat-leaf parsley

1 cup (60 g) chopped fresh mint

5 green onions, white and tender green parts, thinly sliced

⅓ cup (80 ml) fresh lemon juice (about 3 lemons)

2 tablespoons extra-virgin olive oil

1 teaspoon fine sea salt

½ cup (75 g) golden raisins or dried currants

½ cup (70 g) pistachios, toasted and coarsely chopped

Romaine hearts or Little Gem lettuce lettuces, for serving

turkey salad with grapes, pomegranate arils, and pistachios Serves 4

Pistachios are harvested in early fall, the same time table grapes are ripe and pomegranates are turning red on the trees, making this recipe a seasonal celebration. Tossed with a creamy dressing, the salad is served on a bed of red radicchio and arugula leaves, heightening both the flavor and fall color of the dish.

FOR THE DRESSING:

½ cup (50 g) grated Parmesan cheese

3 tablespoons extra-virgin olive oil

2 tablespoons red wine vinegar

8 ounces (225 g) large, red seedless grapes, halved

½ cup (70 g) whole pistachios, plus ⅓ cup (40 g) coarsely chopped

½ cup (85 g) pomegranate arils (seeds), plus 3 tablespoons for garnish

1½ pounds (680 g) roasted turkey breast, cut or torn into bite-size pieces

1 small head radicchio

1 cup (20 g) arugula leaves

Make the dressing: In a small bowl, whisk together cheese, oil, and vinegar until creamy.

In a large bowl, combine the grapes, whole pistachios, pomegranate arils, and turkey. Pour the dressing over the salad and toss to coat well.

Separate the radicchio into individual leaves or coarsely chop the whole head on a cutting board, as desired. On a serving platter, toss together the radicchio and arugula to make a bed. Spoon the salad on top. Garnish with the chopped pistachios and reserved pomegranate arils and serve.

grilled little gem salad with avocado and pistachio-parmesan dressing   Serves 4

The nutty, slightly smoky flavor of grilled Little Gems makes an inspired pairing with the salty pistachio-Parmesan dressing, one that would also welcome the addition of grilled chicken or shrimp to make a main course salad. Serve with crispy pita chips or garlic croutons.

In a food processor, combine whole pistachios, cheese, and salt and process until a loose paste forms. With the processor running, drizzle in 5 tablespoons (75 ml) of the oil and the lemon juice to make a dressing. Set the dressing aside.

Preheat a stovetop grill pan over medium-high heat. While the pan is heating, gently brush the halved lettuce heads with the remaining 1 tablespoon oil. When the grill pan is hot, place the lettuce halves, cut side down, on the pan and grill until the edges are lightly golden, about 2 minutes. Turn and grill the second side until lightly golden, about 2 minutes longer.

Place the lettuce halves on four salad plates. Drizzle each half with some of the dressing. Top with the avocado pieces, dividing them evenly, then drizzle with more dressing. Sprinkle with the chopped pistachios and serve with pita chips.

⅓ cup (45 g) whole pistachios, plus 2 tablespoons chopped

½ cup (50 g) grated Parmesan cheese

½ teaspoon fine sea salt

6 tablespoons (90 ml) extra-virgin olive oil

1½ tablespoons fresh lemon juice

2 heads Little Gem lettuce, halved lengthwise

2 avocados, pitted, peeled, and cubed or sliced

Pita chips, for serving

moroccan citrus salad
with beets, pistachios, mint,
and pistachio oil Serves 4

Citrus salads are popular throughout Morocco, offering a vibrant accompaniment to spicy stews and grilled meats. They require little dressing, usually just a drizzle of oil, letting the citrus juices flavor the dish. Here, the addition of sweet roasted beets, salty olives, and buttery pistachios creates a jewel-toned variation on the classic citrus salad. Garnish with the nuts just before serving to preserve their crunch.

5 or 6 medium beets, preferably a mixture of colors

2 to 3 tablespoons pistachio oil

2 large navel oranges

Small mint sprigs, for garnish

¼ teaspoon fine sea salt

12 pitted green olives, halved

⅓ cup (45 g) pistachios, toasted and coarsely chopped

Freshly ground black pepper

Preheat the oven to 350°F (175°C).

If the beet greens are still attached, cut them off, leaving about ¼ inch (6 mm) of the stem attached, and reserve the greens for another use. Then trim off the root from each beet, again leaving a small bit attached. Rub the beets with a little of the oil, place them in a shallow baking dish, and cover with foil. Roast the beets until they can be easily pierced with a fork, about 50 minutes. Let cool until they can be handled, then rub each beet with a paper towel to remove the skin. Let the beets cool completely, trim off any remaining stem or root, and cut crosswise into slices ¼ inch (6 mm) thick.

While the beets are roasting, prepare the oranges. Cut a thin slice off both ends of 1 orange and stand the orange upright on a cutting board. Using a serrated knife, cut downward, following the curve of the orange and rotating the orange after each cut, to remove the peel and white pith in wide strips. Repeat with the second orange. Cut the oranges crosswise into slices ¼ inch (6 mm) thick.

On a serving platter, arrange the beets and oranges, alternating the slices. There will be more beet slices than orange. Tuck in a few mint sprigs. Drizzle with the remaining oil, sprinkle with the salt, and scatter the olives on top. Finish with the pistachios and a few grinds of pepper and serve.

A Middle Eastern Love Affair with Pistachios

This is a love letter to pistachios, without which Lebanese cuisine—and cuisines throughout the Middle East—would be incomplete, forlorn! With such good reason: pistachio nuts are the "ten" of nuts, presenting the cook and the consumer with everything they desire. Start with the most important aspect of any ingredient, which is flavor. That delicate, buttery pistachio flavor leans savory or sweet with ease. Eaten out of hand, pistachios are ultra-satisfying and healthy. Who doesn't love to leisurely snap open a salty pistachio, savoring the prize, and go back quickly for the next one?! Pistachio texture is equally exceptional, yielding a satisfying crunch whether the nut is whole or crushed, roasted or raw. But the magnetism of pistachios that is most magical for me is the color. That green! Raw pistachios are a feast for the eyes and a ground topping we use to lovingly finish sweets wherever possible in the Lebanese repertoire. Dear pistachio, you do it all . . . you gild the lily . . . you are a casual feast . . . we love you so . . .

—MAUREEN ABOOD, author of the award-winning cookbook *Rose Water & Orange Blossoms: Fresh and Classic Recipes from My Lebanese Kitchen,* and more at www.maureenabood.com

blistered green beans and cherry tomatoes with pistachio pesto Serves 4

2 tablespoons extra-virgin olive oil

1 pound (455 g) green beans, trimmed

1 cup (170 g) cherry tomatoes, in a mixture of colors

½ teaspoon fine sea salt

½ cup (120 g) Pistachio Pesto (page 72)

This colorful side dish is a play on the classic pasta al pesto genovese, which includes cooked potatoes and green beans. Here, the beans are given center stage—no pasta required— blistering them until they are slightly smoky along with cherry tomatoes and then tossing them with pesto made with buttery pistachios. It makes a terrific one-pan side to serve with fish or meat, or it can be topped with a fried egg for brunch. To ensure the beans cook properly, dry them well after rinsing.

In a frying pan large enough to hold all the beans in a single layer, heat the oil over medium-high heat. When the oil is hot, add the beans and cook without stirring until lightly browned and blistered, about 3 minutes. Turn and repeat until the second side is lightly browned and blistered, 1 to 2 minutes longer. Transfer the beans to a platter.

Return the pan to medium-high heat, add the tomatoes, and cook, turning occasionally, until they blister and pop, about 2 minutes. Spoon them over the green beans and sprinkle with the salt. Top with the pesto in small spoonfuls and serve.

potato salad with pistachios, celery, and preserved lemon Serves 4

Thought to have originated in North Africa, preserved lemons—sometimes called lemon pickle—are lemons preserved in their own juice and salt. They are easy to make at home and take about three weeks to cure but are now widely available in well-stocked markets and from specialty retailers. They add a salty, lemony bite to stews, roasted meats and fish, and vegetable dishes that's hard to resist. Here, combined with pistachios, they make an everyday potato salad sing! Add more preserved lemon and pistachios as desired.

In a large saucepan, combine the potatoes with water to cover by 2 inches (5 cm) and bring to a boil over medium-high heat. Reduce the heat to medium and cook just until tender when pierced with a fork, about 20 minutes. Drain well. When cool enough to handle, cut into rounds ½ inch (12 mm) thick. Set aside.

In a large bowl, combine the oil, vinegar, preserved lemon, salt, pepper, diced celery, pistachios, and about two-thirds of the celery leaves and mix well. Add the still-warm potatoes and turn gently to coat with the seasonings. Cover and let stand at room temperature for 45 minutes to allow the flavors to blend. Then refrigerate for several more hours or overnight before serving.

When ready to serve, taste and adjust the seasoning with salt and pepper if needed. Garnish with the remaining celery leaves and serve chilled.

Note: To prep the preserved lemon, rinse off the excess salt, scrape away the pulp, and chop the peel. You can discard the pulp or save it for use in soups or stews.

1 pound (455 g) medium red potatoes

¼ cup (60 ml) extra-virgin olive oil

3 tablespoons white wine vinegar

5 tablespoons (30 g) chopped preserved lemon peel (see Note)

½ teaspoon fine sea salt

¼ teaspoon freshly ground black pepper

2 cups (200 g) diced celery (about 5 medium stalks)

⅓ cup (45 g) pistachios, toasted and chopped

⅓ cup (15 g) chopped celery leaves

grilled asparagus with sieved egg and pistachio oil vinaigrette

Serves 3 or 4

Using pistachio oil for the vinaigrette and finishing the dish with chopped pistachios creates a contemporary version of the French classic asparagus mimosa. The term mimosa *means a dish with hard-cooked eggs, and this dish, in its purest version, is topped with egg whites and yolks sieved or chopped separately. Served in bistros and homes all over France, it makes an ideal accompaniment to baked ham or roast chicken or a welcome first course on its own.*

Preheat a stovetop grill pan over high heat. Meanwhile, brush the asparagus with the olive oil. When the pan is hot, add the asparagus and cook, turning often, until the stalks become a bright green and offer only slight resistance when pierced with a fork, about 5 minutes. Transfer the asparagus to a side plate.

Make the vinaigrette: In a bowl, whisk together the pistachio oil and mustard until emulsified. Whisk in the vinegar, salt, and pepper. Taste and adjust the seasoning if needed.

Pool half of the vinaigrette onto the center of a serving platter or divide evenly among three or four salad plates. Top with the warm asparagus. Drizzle with some of the remaining vinaigrette.

Peel the eggs and cut in half crosswise. Scoop the yolk from each half. Using a small fine-mesh sieve, and holding it over the center of the asparagus, push the egg whites through the mesh. You will need to scrape the bottom of the sieve to release all the whites. Repeat with the egg yolks. Sprinkle the pistachios on top and serve.

1 pound (455 g) asparagus, trimmed

2 tablespoons extra-virgin olive oil

FOR THE VINAIGRETTE:

¼ cup (60 ml) pistachio oil

1 teaspoon Dijon mustard

1 tablespoon red wine vinegar

¼ teaspoon fine sea salt

⅛ teaspoon white pepper

2 hard-cooked eggs

¼ cup (35 g) pistachios, toasted and coarsely chopped

roasted delicata squash with harissa yogurt and pistachios

Serves 4

This is a handsome side dish to accompany chicken or pork, or it can be paired with couscous or quinoa for a vegetarian main course. Available from summer through early winter, delicata squash sports edible, yellow-and-green-striped skin. Harissa, a North African chile paste that is also popular in France, is mixed into yogurt to make a tangy hot sauce that can be drizzled or spooned over the roasted squash.

2 delicata squashes (about 1 pound /454 g each)

2 tablespoons extra-virgin olive oil

½ teaspoon fine sea salt

¼ teaspoon freshly ground black pepper

½ teaspoon harissa or other chile paste

½ cup (100 g) plain Greek yogurt (whole milk, low-fat, or nonfat)

½ cup (85 g) pomegranate arils

½ cup (70 g) pistachios, coarsely chopped

Small cilantro sprigs, for garnish

Preheat the oven to 400°F (200°C). Line a sheet pan with parchment paper.

Trim off both ends from each squash and set aside. Using a metal spoon, scoop out and discard the seeds from each squash. Cut the squashes into a mix of rings 1 inch (2.5 cm) thick and chunky wedges. Cut some of the rings in half. Transfer all the squash pieces to a large bowl. Trim away the stem and blossom portions from the reserved ends and add the ends to the bowl.

Drizzle the squash pieces with the oil and toss to coat evenly. Turn the squash pieces out onto the prepared sheet pan and spread in a single layer. Season with half each of the salt and pepper. Turn the pieces and season the second side with the remaining salt and pepper.

Roast the squash pieces until golden brown, about 20 minutes. Turn and roast until golden brown and just tender when pierced with a fork, about 15 minutes longer. Turn off the oven and let the squash sit in the oven for 5 minutes before serving.

While the squash is roasting, in a small serving bowl, stir the harissa into the yogurt, mixing well.

To serve, transfer the squash pieces to a platter and scatter the pomegranate arils and pistachios over the top. Garnish with the cilantro and set the bowl of harissa yogurt alongside.

sicilian roasted cauliflower with pistachios, capers, and olives Serves 6

The island of Pantelleria, off the coast of Sicily, is famous for its wild capers, which are sold packed in sea salt. Sicilian olives are said to be flavored by the sea air, and the pistachios from the trees growing on the island's volcanic slopes are so prized that the orchards are guarded against thieves. The taste of Sicily imbues this trio of ingredients used as a topping for a whole roasted cauliflower in this glorious dish. Serve and carve it right at the table. It's a side dish your guests cannot refuse.

Preheat the oven to 375°F (190°C).

Remove any green leaves and stems from the cauliflower. Carefully slice off the stem end so the cauliflower will stand upright.

Rub the cauliflower all over with the oil and then with the salt. Stand it in a baking dish or cast-iron frying pan and roast until golden brown and easily pierced with a fork, about 1 hour.

While the cauliflower is roasting, make the topping. In a bowl, whisk together the oil, lemon juice, capers, and salt to make a sauce.

When the cauliflower is ready, remove from the oven. Leave the hot cauliflower in its baking dish or frying pan or transfer to a serving platter. Pour the sauce over the top, then sprinkle with the olives and pistachios. Cut into wedges to serve.

Note: If using salt-packed capers, rinse off the salt, then soak in a small bowl of cold water to cover for about 2 minutes and drain. If using brined capers, drain well before measuring.

1 head cauliflower

2 tablespoons extra-virgin olive oil

½ teaspoon fine sea salt

FOR THE TOPPING:

½ cup (120 ml) extra-virgin olive oil

2 tablespoons fresh lemon juice

2 tablespoons capers (see Note)

½ teaspoon fine sea salt

½ cup (70 g) pitted green olives, sliced

⅓ cup (45 g) pistachios, toasted and coarsely chopped

persian rice with pistachios and saffron   Serves 6 to 8

Rice pilaf, one of the most popular dishes in Persian cooking, has many variations, some of which include pistachios and saffron, as in this recipe. The sweet and tart flavors of barberries and orange zest add a surprising bite to this colorful dish. It's traditionally served alongside stews, but it's also a fine accompaniment to grilled meat and poultry.

½ teaspoon saffron threads

6 tablespoons (90 ml) hot water

3 tablespoons dried barberries (see Note)

2 tablespoons unsalted butter

1 teaspoon ground cardamom

1 cinnamon stick (2 inches/5 cm)

2 cups (360 g) long-grain white rice

3½ cups (840 ml) chicken broth or water

2 teaspoons fine sea salt

3 teaspoons freshly grated orange zest

2 tablespoons golden raisins

⅓ cup (45 g) pistachios, toasted

In a small bowl, combine the saffron and 2 tablespoons of the hot water and set aside until ready to use. In a second small bowl, combine the barberries and the remaining 4 tablespoons (60 ml) hot water and let soak for 15 minutes. Drain well, leaving any grit in the bottom of bowl behind. Set aside.

In a saucepan, melt the butter over medium-high heat. When the butter foams, add the cardamom and cinnamon stick and stir for 1 minute. Add the rice and cook, stirring, until a little of the rice browns, about 3 minutes.

Add the broth, salt, the saffron and its soaking water, and half of the orange zest and stir well. Bring to a boil, reduce the heat to low, cover, and cook until the rice is nearly tender, about 20 minutes.

Remove and discard the cinnamon stick. Sprinkle the rice with the raisins and drained barberries, re-cover, and cook for another 5 minutes.

To serve, stir three-fourths of the pistachios into the rice. Transfer the rice to a serving bowl or platter and garnish with the remaining orange zest and pistachios.

Note: Small, red, tangy barberries are a popular addition to pilaf, chicken salad, or lamb stuffing. They are sold dried in packages in Middle Eastern groceries and online.

main courses

orecchiette with spring asparagus, peas, and ricotta with pistachio pesto   Serves 4 to 6

The little cup-like rounds of chewy, plump orecchiette—"little ears" in Italian—are ideal for catching the creamy ricotta and nut-laden pesto that comprise the sauce for this hearty spring dish. Use the freshest young asparagus and peas you can find. If fresh peas aren't available, frozen baby peas can be substituted.

1 tablespoon extra-virgin olive oil

12 ounces (340 g) thin or medium asparagus, trimmed and cut into 1-inch (2.5-cm) lengths

2 teaspoons fine sea salt, plus more if needed

12 ounces (340 g) orecchiette

1 cup (145 g) shelled fresh peas or frozen baby peas

⅔ cup (160 g) Pistachio Pesto (page 72)

1 cup (240 g) whole-milk ricotta cheese

¼ cup (25 g) grated pecorino romano cheese

In a large frying pan, heat the oil over medium-high heat. When the oil is hot, add the asparagus pieces and cook, turning them several times, until they are bright green and offer little resistance when pierced with a fork, about 3 minutes for thin stalks and 5 minutes for medium stalks. Set aside.

Meanwhile, bring a large pot of water to a boil. Add the salt and the pasta, stir well, and cook until al dente, according to the package directions. During the last minute of cooking, add the peas to the pot. Drain well.

Transfer the pasta and peas to a warmed, large serving bowl or platter and add the asparagus. Add the pesto and toss gently to coat evenly. Taste and adjust the seasoning with salt if needed. Dot with spoonfuls of half of the ricotta and sprinkle with the pecorino romano. Serve immediately, with the remaining ricotta on the side.

potato saffron tart with pistachios and golden raisins

Serves 6 as a main course, or 8 as a side dish

1½ cups (360 ml) heavy cream

¼ teaspoon saffron threads

2 pounds (910 g) Yukon Gold or other firm-fleshed potato

2 sheets tart or pie pastry for a double-crust 10-inch (25-cm) tart, homemade or purchased

1 tablespoon fine sea salt

½ teaspoon white pepper

1 tablespoon fresh oregano leaves

3 tablespoons golden raisins

¾ cup (105 g) pistachios, toasted and chopped

1 large egg yolk mixed with 1 tablespoon water

This rich, creamy potato tart with its flaky crust is redolent with the flavors of saffron, pistachio, and golden raisins. It makes an excellent main course for brunch or lunch alongside a green salad, and it can also be served cold as picnic fare with roast beef, horseradish, and perhaps a glass of Champagne.

Preheat the oven to 425°F (220°C).

In a saucepan, bring the cream to a simmer over medium heat. Remove from the heat, transfer 2 tablespoons to a small bowl, and add the saffron to the bowl. Set the bowl with the saffron and the pan of cream aside.

Using a mandoline or a sharp knife, cut the potatoes crosswise into thin slices.

Line a 10-inch (25-cm) tart pan with a removable bottom with a pastry sheet, pressing it onto the bottom and up the sides and letting the edges overlap the rim of the pan. Layer half of the potato slices in the pastry-lined pan. Sprinkle with half each of the salt, pepper, oregano, raisins, and pistachios. Repeat the layers.

Stir the saffron and its cream into the saucepan of cream. If the cream has cooled, reheat over medium heat to just below a simmer. Pour the hot cream over the potatoes, lifting the slices a bit to allow the cream to reach through all the layers.

Top with the second pastry sheet and trim the overhang of both sheets to about ½ inch (12 mm). Fold the edge of the sheets together underneath themselves and even with the pan rim, then pinch together to seal securely. Using a small, sharp knife, cut three or four slits in the top crust to allow steam to escape. With a pastry brush, brush the entire top crust with the egg yolk–water mixture.

Bake for 10 minutes, then adjust the oven control to 350°F (175°C) and continue to bake until the crust is golden and a knife slipped through a slit into the center comes out clean, 35 to 40 minutes.

Let the tart cool on a wire rack for 10 minutes. Then, using the tip of a knife, loosen the edges of the crust from the tart ring. Set the tart pan on an inverted small bowl and gently slide the tart ring downward away from the crust. Place the tart, still on the pan bottom, on a serving plate. Cut into wedges and serve warm.

tuna poke with seaweed salad, pistachios, and wonton chips

Serves 4 as a main course, or 8 as an appetizer

Poke, the popular Hawaiian dish of chopped raw tuna dressed with soy and sesame oil, has become a staple on the mainland of California and elsewhere. If nuts are used, the macadamia is the Hawaiian choice, but pistachios add an equal crunch and a slightly different flavor. The wontons can be served separately or tucked into the poke. For maximum freshness, buy the ahi tuna frozen and let it thaw in your refrigerator at your convenience, then proceed with the recipe.

Line a large platter with paper towels and set it near the stove. Pour the neutral oil to a depth of 1½ to 2 inches (4 to 5 cm) into a deep sauté pan. Heat over medium-high heat to 350°F (175°C) on a deep-frying thermometer or until a scrap of wonton wrapper dropped into the oil bubbles on contact.

When the oil is ready, add the wonton pieces a few at a time, being careful not to crowd the pan, and fry until lightly golden on the first side, about 1 minute. Using tongs, turn and fry the second side until lightly golden, 30 to 45 seconds longer. Use the tongs to transfer the wonton pieces to the towel-lined platter to drain. Repeat until all the wonton pieces are fried, reducing the heat if they are browning too quickly.

Cut the tuna into small dice. In a large bowl, stir together the soy sauce, sesame oil, and vinegar. Add the tuna and turn several times to coat with the mixture. Gently fold in the green onions, the avocado, and half of the seaweed salad, mixing well.

Spoon the tuna mixture onto a serving platter or individual plates. Scatter the pistachios over the top and spoon the remaining seaweed salad alongside. Garnish with the wonton chips and serve immediately.

Neutral oil, such as grapeseed or canola, for deep-frying

8 wonton wrappers, each cut into 6 diamond-shaped pieces

1⅓ pounds (600 g) sashimi-grade ahi (yellowfin) tuna

2½ tablespoons soy sauce

2½ teaspoons Asian sesame oil

1 teaspoon rice vinegar

4 green onions, white and tender green parts, minced

1 avocado, pitted, peeled, and diced

8 ounces (225 g) seaweed salad

½ cup (70 g) pistachios, toasted

pistachio butter–basted shrimp tacos

Make 8 tacos; serves 4

Nutty-flavored pistachio butter is the secret sauce for these quick and easy shrimp tacos. Keeping the extras to a minimum—just a little shredded cabbage, cilantro, green onions for crunch, and a drizzle of crema—allows the shrimp, with its unusual chili powder–pistachio flavor, to take center stage.

Preheat the oven to 250°F (120°C).

Lay a slightly damp kitchen towel near the stove. Preheat a griddle or frying pan over medium-high heat. When it is hot, add a tortilla and heat until almost soft, about 30 seconds. Turn and heat for 30 seconds on the second side. Transfer to one end of the towel and cover with the other end. Repeat until all the tortillas have been warmed, then wrap in the towel, place on a sheet pan or oven-safe dish, and place in the oven until ready to use.

In a frying pan large enough to hold all the shrimp in a single layer, heat the oil over medium-high heat. When the oil is hot, add the shrimp, sprinkle them evenly with the chili powder and salt, and cook, turning once, until just pink and curled, about 2 minutes total. Add the pistachio butter to the pan and, as it melts, baste the shrimp with it. Remove from the heat.

Remove the tortillas from the oven, unwrap them, and arrange them on a work surface. Divide the shrimp, cabbage, green onions, and avocado evenly among the warm tortillas. Place the tacos on a large platter and spoon a little crema on each taco, if desired. Garnish with cilantro sprigs and lime wedges and serve.

8 (6-inch/15-cm) corn tortillas

1½ tablespoons extra-virgin olive oil

1 pound (455 g) large shrimp (about 25), peeled and deveined

1 teaspoon chili powder

¼ teaspoon fine sea salt

2 tablespoons pistachio butter

1 cup (70 g) finely shredded purple cabbage

6 green onions, white and tender green parts, thinly sliced

1 avocado, pitted, peeled, and thinly sliced

⅓ cup (80 ml) crema or (75 g) crème fraîche (optional)

1 cup (55 g) loosely packed fresh cilantro sprigs

2 limes, quartered

swordfish with smoky cherry tomato–pistachio salsa Serves 4

FOR THE SALSA:

1 tablespoon pistachio or extra-virgin olive oil

2½ teaspoons sherry vinegar

1 clove garlic, crushed and minced

½ teaspoon Spanish smoked paprika

¼ teaspoon fine sea salt

2 cups (340 g) cherry tomatoes, in a mixture of colors, halved

½ cup (90 g) finely chopped red onion

¼ cup (35 g) pistachios, coarsely chopped

4 swordfish steaks, about ½ inch (12 mm) thick (about 5½ ounces/155 g each)

½ teaspoon fine sea salt

½ teaspoon freshly ground black pepper

2 tablespoons unsalted butter

A hint of Spanish smoked paprika lends an unexpected fragrance to this bright, refreshing salsa, which enhances the meaty richness of the swordfish. The salsa also makes a good topping for other white-fleshed fish or for sautéed chicken breasts or thighs. Tabbouleh with Pistachios and Golden Raisins (page 89) or Persian Rice with Pistachios and Saffron (page 102) would be a good accompaniment to the swordfish.

Make the salsa: In a bowl, combine the oil, vinegar, garlic, paprika, and salt and mix well. Add the tomatoes, onion, and pistachios and stir to coat evenly with the oil mixture. Set aside.

Season the fish steaks on both sides with the salt and pepper. In a frying pan large enough to hold the fish steaks in a single layer, melt the butter over medium-high heat. When the butter foams, add the fish steaks and cook until the bottoms are golden and the sides are beginning to become opaque, about 3 minutes. Turn and continue to cook until golden on the second side, the sides are completely opaque, and the flesh easily flakes with a fork, about 4 minutes longer.

Transfer the fish steaks to dinner plates. Spoon the salsa over the steaks, dividing it evenly. Serve immediately.

Note: If possible, assemble the salsa, except for adding the pistachios, an hour in advance of serving, and let sit at room temperature to allow the flavors to mingle. Then stir in the pistachios when ready to serve.

pan-seared cod with
pistachio-orange beurre blanc Serves 4

FOR THE BEURRE BLANC:

1 orange

⅛ teaspoon fine sea salt

¼ cup (60 ml) heavy cream

2 to 3 tablespoons unsalted butter

⅓ cup (45 g) pistachios, toasted
and finely chopped

4 cod fillets, each ½ to 1 inch
(12 mm to 2.5 cm) thick (about
5½ ounces/155 g each)

1 teaspoon fine sea salt

1 teaspoon freshly ground black
pepper

1 tablespoon fresh lemon juice

1 tablespoon unsalted butter

1 tablespoon extra-virgin olive oil

Beurre blanc is a classic French butter-based emulsified sauce made with a little white wine, white wine vinegar, cream, and shallot. The delicate sauce is ideal for mild-flavored fish like cod, trout, and haddock because it doesn't overwhelm them. But other flavors and ingredients can be added to give the sauce a modern twist.

Here, the shallots have been omitted, the wine and vinegar have been swapped out for orange juice and zest, and pistachios have been added for texture. The sauce is also excellent on shellfish, such as lobster and scallops.

Make the beurre blanc: Grate 1 tablespoon zest from the orange and set aside. Cut the orange in half, and squeeze the juice from one half into a small saucepan. Bring the juice to a boil over medium-high heat. Reduce the heat to medium and stir in the salt and cream. Simmer, stirring, until thickened, about 5 minutes. Reduce the heat to low and add the orange zest, and simmer for 1 to 2 minutes. Stir in 2 tablespoons of the butter and all but 1 tablespoon of the pistachios until the butter melts. If you like, stir in the remaining 1 tablespoon butter until melted. Remove from the heat and cover to keep warm.

Put the cod fillets into a large bowl and sprinkle with the salt, pepper, and lemon juice, turning the fillets several times to coat.

In a frying pan large enough to hold the fish fillets in a single layer, melt the butter with the oil over medium-high heat. Add the fish fillets and cook until the bottoms are golden and the sides are beginning to become opaque, about 5 minutes. Turn and cook until the second side is golden, the sides are completely opaque, and the flesh flakes easily with a fork, about 4 minutes longer.

Transfer the fish to dinner plates or shallow bowls. Drizzle the warm sauce over and around each serving. Garnish with the remaining 1 tablespoon pistachios and serve at once.

chicken milanese with pistachio-parmesan crust Serves 4

Traditionally made with veal, cotoletta alla milanese is a classic northern Italian dish from the region of Lombardy. Veal cutlets or chops are pounded until quite thin, then dredged in bread crumbs and quickly panfried in butter. Over time, other meats, such as pork and chicken, have been prepared in a similar way, and the result, despite the simplicity of the preparation, is equally spectacular.

To make the chicken cutlets extra crispy and even more flavorful, the coating is made with panko mixed with ground pistachios and a little grated Parmesan. Serve the chicken on its own, the traditional way, with lemon wedges, or with a side of sautéed spinach or other greens.

1½ pounds (680 g) large skinless, boneless chicken breast halves

1½ cups (190 g) all-purpose flour

1 teaspoon fine sea salt

½ teaspoon freshly ground black pepper

1 cup (65 g) panko

1 cup (140 g) pistachios, finely chopped

½ cup (50 g) grated Parmesan cheese

3 large eggs

4 tablespoons (55 g) unsalted butter

4 tablespoons (60 ml) extra-virgin olive oil

1 lemon, cut into 4 wedges

Preheat the oven to 225°F (110°C).

Holding a chicken breast down with one hand, and using a sharp knife, split the breast lengthwise into halves. Repeat with the remaining breasts.

On a work surface, lay the breast pieces, two at a time and spaced well apart, between two sheets of plastic wrap. With a flat meat mallet or a heavy frying pan, pound the pieces until they are evenly thin and nearly double their original size. Set aside and repeat with the remaining split breasts.

Lay two large sheets of waxed paper or plastic wrap on a work surface. In a shallow bowl, whisk together the flour, salt, and pepper, then turn the seasoned flour out onto one of the sheets. In the same bowl, whisk together the panko, pistachios, and Parmesan, then turn the mixture out onto the second sheet. In the same bowl, whisk the eggs until blended and set the bowl between the flour and panko mixtures. Set a large platter and a sheet pan near the panko mixture.

Preheat a large frying pan over medium-high heat. While the pan is heating, one at a time, dredge the chicken cutlets in the seasoned flour, coating both sides and shaking off the excess, and then dip into the egg, allowing the excess to drip back into bowl. Finally, gently press both sides into the panko mixture, covering evenly and shaking off the excess, then set aside on the platter.

When the frying pan is hot, melt the butter with the oil. When they are hot, place 3 or 4 cutlets, depending on their size, into the pan. Fry until golden on the first side, about 4 minutes. Turn and fry the second side until golden, about 3 minutes longer. Transfer to the sheet pan and keep warm in the oven. Repeat until all the cutlets are cooked.

Serve the cutlets immediately with the lemon wedges.

afghan-style chicken and rice with candied citrus and pistachios   Serves 4 to 6

Rice is the centerpiece of the Afghan table. Its presentation ranges from steamed to gloriously garnished with vegetables, fruits, nuts, and meats. This dish is inspired by Kabuli palaw, the national dish of Afghanistan, which is chicken or lamb tucked into seasoned rice and garnished with carrots, raisins, and nuts. Although the recipe calls for a long list of ingredients and has several steps, the dish is easy to cook and assemble, and the flavors and presentation are well worth the effort.

Preheat the oven to 350°F (175°C).

In a small bowl, combine the saffron and hot water and set aside.

Season the chicken thighs on all sides with 1 teaspoon of the salt and the pepper. In a Dutch oven or deep, oven-safe frying pan, heat the oil over medium-high heat. When the oil is hot, add the chicken and cook until golden on the underside, about 5 minutes. Turn and cook the second side until golden, about 4 minutes longer. Transfer to a large plate and set aside.

Return the pan to medium-high heat and add the butter. When the butter has melted, add the onion, reduce the heat to medium, and cook, stirring often, until the onion is soft, about 10 minutes. Add the garlic and the garam masala and stir to mix. Add the tomato paste and cook, stirring, for 30 seconds. Raise the heat to medium-high and slowly add the broth, stirring to loosen any clinging browned bits on the pot bottom. Add the saffron and its water, stir to mix, and then add the remaining 1 teaspoon salt. Bring to a boil.

Add the rice and any collected juices from the chicken, stir to mix, and then level the rice in the pot. Return the chicken to the pot, tucking it into the rice. Cover the pot and transfer to the oven. Bake until most of the liquid is absorbed and the rice is nearly tender, about 45 minutes. Remove from the oven, top with the raisins and carrots, cover, and return to the oven for another 5 minutes to finish cooking the rice and to warm the raisins and carrots.

To serve, heap onto a serving platter, keeping the raisins and carrots on top. Garnish with the candied orange peel and pistachios and serve.

¼ teaspoon saffron threads

2 tablespoons hot water

6 skin-on, bone-in chicken thighs

2 teaspoons fine sea salt

½ teaspoon freshly ground black pepper

1 teaspoon extra-virgin olive oil

3 tablespoons unsalted butter

1 yellow onion, chopped

2 cloves garlic, minced

2 teaspoons garam marsala

2 tablespoons tomato paste

4 cups (960 ml) chicken broth

2 cups (360 g) basmati rice

2 tablespoons raisins or dried currants

2 carrots, peeled and cut into matchstick strips 2 inches by ¼ inch (5 cm by 6 mm)

2 tablespoons chopped candied orange peel or dried apricot

¼ cup (35 g) pistachios, coarsely chopped

roast quail with fig and pistachio stuffing Serves 4

4 plump quail (about 4 ounces/115 g each), preferably partially boned

2 tablespoons unsalted butter, at room temperature (optional)

2 teaspoons coarse sea salt

2 teaspoons freshly ground black pepper

4 thyme sprigs, plus 1 tablespoon fresh thyme leaves

3 thick slices bâtard or other country-style bread, or 6 slices baguette

¼ cup finely chopped yellow onion

4 dried figs

¼ cup (27 g) pistachio meal

¼ cup (25 g) finely chopped pistachios

½ cup (120 ml) dry white wine

½ to 1 tablespoon balsamic vinegar

Quail, a small game bird with a mild flavor and firm flesh, is perfect for stuffing with this eastern Mediterranean–inspired mixture of figs and pistachios. A platter of these little birds makes a casual yet impressive main course. Roasted Delicata Squash with Harissa Yogurt and Pistachios (page 98) and creamy polenta or light, fluffy couscous would be fine accompaniments.

Preheat the oven to 375°F (190°C).

Pat the quail dry with paper towels. Cut 1 tablespoon of the butter in half. Rub ½ tablespoon all over the outside of the quail. Cut the remaining ½ tablespoon into quarters and put a quarter into the cavity of each bird. In a small bowl, stir together the salt and pepper. Rub half of the mixture inside the cavity and on the outside of all the quail. Tuck a thyme sprig into each cavity.

Trim the crusts off the bread slices, then tear the bread into 1-inch (2.5-cm) pieces and place in a bowl. Add the remaining salt and pepper mixture, the onion, and the thyme leaves. Trim the tough stem end off of each fig, then cut the figs into ½-inch (1.25-cm) pieces. Add to the bread mixture, and toss to mix. Add the pistachio meal and the chopped pistachios and mix again. Stuff about one-fourth of the mixture into each bird, making sure each portion includes some fig pieces. Truss the legs with kitchen string.

Place the quail, breast side up, on a sheet pan. Cut the remaining 1 tablespoon room-temperature butter into small bits and dot the birds with the butter.

Roast the quail, using a pastry brush to baste them with the pan juices three or four times during cooking, until the juices run clear when a thigh is pierced with the tip of a knife, 15 to 20 minutes.

Transfer the quail to a cutting board, tent loosely with aluminum foil, and let rest for 10 minutes.

To make the pan sauce, place the sheet pan on the stovetop and turn on the heat to medium-high. Pour in the wine and scrape up any clinging browned bits on the pan bottom. Cook down a bit to thicken, then add the vinegar to taste. For a richer, more velvety sauce, stir in the 2 tablespoons butter.

Snip and remove the kitchen string on each quail. If desired, using poultry shears, cut each quail in half lengthwise and place the halves on a serving platter. Or serve the quail whole on four dinner plates. Drizzle with the pan sauce and serve immediately.

seared duck breast with fresh cherries and pistachios Serves 4

Duck with cherries was a fine-dining favorite of yesteryear, popular in restaurants lined with heavy velvet drapes and where silent servers lifted silver domes in unison for the reveal. In this contemporary version, seared duck breasts are paired with a quick sauce of fresh cherries and pistachios—no silver dome needed.

Make the sauce: In a saucepan, heat the oil over medium-high heat. When the oil is hot, add the onion and celery and cook, stirring, until the onion is nearly translucent, about 2 minutes. Set aside about ¼ cup (40 g) of the cherries and add the remainder to the pan along with the vinegar and ginger. Reduce the heat to medium and continue to cook, stirring and pressing against the cherries with the back of a wooden spoon, until slightly thickened, 4 to 5 minutes.

Stir in the honey, salt, and half of the pistachios (set aside the remainder for the garnish) and continue to cook, stirring, until the mixture has thickened and the onion, celery, and cherries have somewhat dissolved, 3 to 4 minutes. Remove from the heat, let cool slightly, and then taste and adjust the seasoning with more salt if needed. Set aside until ready to serve

While the sauce is cooking, remove the duck breasts from the refrigerator and bring to room temperature, about 30 minutes.

Using a sharp knife, cut through the skin and fat but not into the meat of each duck breast, creating a crosshatch pattern and making the cuts about ½ inch (12 mm) apart. Pat the meat dry and season the breasts well on both sides with the salt and pepper.

When ready to cook, in a large frying pan, melt the butter over medium-high heat. When the butter is hot, place the duck breasts, skin side down, in the pan. Reduce the heat to medium and cook until the skin is crisp and golden, 6 to 7 minutes. Turn and sear the second side until browned and the meat is cooked medium to medium-rare, 4 to 6 minutes. Using tongs, turn the breasts on their sides to sear those as well. Transfer the breasts to a cutting board (preferably a carving board with a groove to capture the juices) and let rest for 5 minutes before carving into slices ½ inch (12 mm) thick.

While the duck rests, reheat the sauce over low heat, stirring constantly. Add the reserved cherries and stir to coat with the sauce.

To serve, divide the duck slices evenly among four warmed dinner plates. Drizzle with the juices from the cutting board, and then spoon some of the warm cherry sauce over each serving. Garnish with the reserved pistachios.

FOR THE SAUCE:

1 tablespoon grapeseed or canola oil

¼ yellow onion, finely chopped (about ¼ cup/35 g)

1 stalk celery, finely chopped (about ¼ cup/35 g)

1 pound (455 g) cherries, pitted and halved

1 tablespoon sherry vinegar

1-inch (2.5-cm) piece fresh ginger, peeled and grated (about 1 teaspoon)

1 tablespoon honey

¼ teaspoon fine sea salt, plus more if needed

⅓ cup (45 g) pistachios, toasted and chopped

3 skin-on duck breast halves (about 8 ounces/225 g each)

½ teaspoon sea salt

½ teaspoon freshly ground black pepper

1 tablespoon unsalted butter

turkish-style lamb and pistachio kebabs with tomato-chile sauce   Serves 3 or 4

1 pound (455 g) ground lamb

1 teaspoon Ancho chile powder

2 teaspoons ground cumin

½ cup (54 g) pistachio meal

1 teaspoon fine sea salt

1 teaspoon Aleppo pepper, or
    ½ teaspoon freshly ground black
    pepper

1 teaspoon sumac, za'atar, or
    grated zest of 1 lemon

FOR THE SAUCE:

1 cup (200 g) plain Greek yogurt
    (whole milk, low-fat, or nonfat)

1 teaspoon Calabrian or similar
    chile sauce, or as needed

1 tomato, finely chopped

Pita or other flatbread, for serving

Olive oil, for brushing kebobs

Thinly sliced red onion, thinly sliced
    tomato, arugula, cilantro, and/
    or lemon wedges, for garnish
    (optional)

The addition of pistachio meal to these ground-lamb kebabs helps hold all the ingredients together and adds wonderful texture and flavor. Serve the skewers on warm pita or another flatbread. For a savory accompaniment, dress a mixture of arugula and fresh herbs, such as mint, basil, parsley, and/or cilantro, with a little lemon juice and olive oil.

Line a large plate with waxed paper or plastic wrap and set it near your work surface. Have ready six wooden skewers. In a large bowl, combine the lamb, chile powder, cumin, pistachio meal, salt, Aleppo pepper, and sumac and mix well with your hands. Divide the lamb mixture into 6 equal portions. Shape each portion around a skewer, making an oval about 6 inches (15 cm) long and 1½ inches (4 cm) wide. As the skewers are ready, place them on the prepared plate in a single layer. Cover and refrigerate for 4 to 6 hours or up to overnight.

Just before you are ready to cook the kebabs, make the sauce: In a bowl, combine the yogurt, chile sauce, and tomato and mix well. Taste and add more chile sauce to suit your palate. Set aside until ready to serve.

To cook the kebabs, prepare a charcoal or gas grill for cooking over medium-high heat, or preheat a stovetop grill pan over medium-high heat.

To warm the flatbread, wrap in aluminum foil and warm in a preheated 350°F (175°C) oven for about 10 minutes. Alternatively, place them on the hot grill or grill pan before cooking the kebabs, then wrap to keep warm until serving.

When the grill or grill pan is ready, lightly brush the kebobs with oil. Lay the skewers on the grill or grill pan and cook until they release easily from the surface, 2 to 3 minutes. Turn and grill until they release easily from the second side and are cooked through, 2 to 3 minutes longer.

Serve the kebabs immediately atop the warmed flatbread. Accompany with the sauce and with any garnishes you like.

Green Gold in Turkey

The pistachio ("fıstık" in Turkish) is the most praised nut in Turkey, enjoyed as a snack and as a key ingredient in desserts, confections, and in such savory dishes as mezes, kebabs, and pilafs. The pistachio-growing region is in southeastern Turkey; the provinces of Gaziantep (Antep for short), Urfa, and Siirt are the leading producers. The Siirt nuts are plump and round with a satisfying full, nutty flavor, and are preferred roasted as a snack. Antep pistachios are slender and long, tender in taste, and mostly used in sweets, such as Turkish delight and baklava.

Early harvest is the key to flavor, but it also means lower yield, so the nuts from Antep are more expensive. These prized pistachios, which are used in sweets and confections—especially in ice cream and pistachio marzipan (fıstık ezmesi)—are a striking green and have an intense aroma, qualities only possible when the nuts are gathered slightly underripe. The tender little gems (boz fıstık) are as precious to the sweets maker as gold to a jeweler, and are thus nicknamed "green gold" by Turkish locals.

— AYLIN ÖNEY TAN, cookbook author of *A Taste of Sun & Fire*, food writer, columnist, and NTV radio broadcaster of *Bitter, Sweet, and Sour* in Turkey; www.aylinoneytan.com

braised beef short ribs with orange peel, dates, and pistachios Serves 4

In Provence, orange zest is a common addition to beef daubes or other stews. Here, with a nod to the eastern Mediterranean, the zest is combined with dates and pistachios to create a rich, hearty dish for any occasion. A green salad and maybe some pearl couscous or saffron rice are all the accompaniments needed, plus good bread for soaking up the sauce.

Preheat the oven to 325°F (165°C).

Season the meat all over with the salt and pepper.

Tie the thyme, parsley, and bay leaf together with kitchen string to make a bouquet garni. With a sharp knife or vegetable peeler, remove the peel in large pieces from the oranges. Set the bouquet garni and orange peel aside. Reserve the oranges for another use.

In a Dutch oven or other large heavy-bottomed pot, heat the oil over medium-high heat. When the oil is hot, working in batches, add the ribs and brown on all sides, about 4 minutes per batch. Transfer to a plate and repeat until all the ribs are browned.

Reduce the heat to medium and add the garlic halves, cut side down. Add the onion and carrots and then stir. Add the tomato paste and stir. Raise the heat to medium-high and slowly pour in the wine, scraping up any clinging browned bits on the pot bottom. Return the ribs to the pan. Add the broth, bouquet garni, and three-fourths of the orange peel and bring to a boil.

Cover the pot and transfer to the oven. Cook until the meat can easily be cut with a fork, about 3 hours. Turn the meat from time to time and add a little more broth if the liquid is running low. Thirty minutes before the meat is ready, cut the remaining orange peel into thin slivers and add half of it to the pot along with the dates. Set the remaining slivered peel aside.

When the meat is ready, remove the pot from the oven and remove and discard the bouquet garni and, if you wish, the bones.

To serve, mound the dish on a shallow serving platter, spoon with sauce, and garnish with the reserved slivered orange peel, the pistachios, and, if desired, a few sprigs of parsley.

3 pounds (1.4 kg) lean beef short ribs

1½ teaspoons fine sea salt

½ teaspoon freshly ground black pepper

4 thyme sprigs

4 flat-leaf parsley sprigs, plus more for garnish (optional)

1 bay leaf

2 oranges

2 tablespoons extra-virgin olive oil

1 head garlic, halved crosswise

1 yellow onion, chopped

2 carrots, peeled and cut into 1-inch (2.5-cm) lengths

3 tablespoons tomato paste

2 cups (480 ml) dry red wine, such as Zinfandel or Syrah

3 cups (720 ml) beef broth, plus more if needed

8 dates, pitted and chopped

½ cup (70 g) pistachios, coarsely chopped

standing rib pork roast with pistachios and apricot glaze   Serves 4 to 6

FOR THE ROAST:

1 (4-rib) pork rib roast (about 3 pounds/1.4 kg)

4 ripe fresh apricots

6 dried apricot halves

1 tablespoon brandy, plus more if needed

1 teaspoon coarse sea salt

½ teaspoon freshly ground black pepper

¼ cup (25 g) finely chopped pistachios

½ teaspoon dried sage

¼ teaspoon red pepper flakes

1 clove garlic, minced

FOR THE GLAZE:

½ cup (120 ml) dry white wine, such as Chardonnay, plus 2 tablespoons

½ teaspoon dried sage

1 teaspoon honey

3 dried apricot halves, finely chopped

3 ripe fresh apricots, for garnish

¼ cup (25 g) finely chopped pistachios, for garnish

The combination of apricots and pistachios serves as the base for an ever-so-slightly spicy paste spread between the ribs and the meat of this impressive roast. Serve the roast with a slice of Potato Saffron Tart with Pistachios and Golden Raisins (page 108) or oven-roasted vegetables.

Prepare the roast: Ask your butcher to separate the rack of rib bones in a single piece from the meat and then to tie the rack back onto the meat with butcher's twine to keep the original shape of the roast. Alternatively, you can do it yourself at home with a sharp knife, cutting close to the bones as you separate the rack from the meat. In this case, there is no need to tie the bones back on until later.

Preheat the oven to 475°F (245°C).

Pit and chop the fresh apricots and chop all the dried apricots and put them into a small bowl. Add the brandy, half of the salt and black pepper, and all the pistachios, sage, red pepper flakes, and garlic and stir with a fork. Let stand for 30 minutes until the mixture absorbs the brandy. Mash the mixture with the back of the fork to form a paste, adding more brandy if needed to moisten.

Snip the twine holding the bones onto the roast. Rub the meat and bones well with the remaining salt and pepper, adding a little more if you like. With the "bone side" of the meat facing you, pack it with the apricot paste. A second pair of hands is useful for this next step. Place the ribs back in place, making sure they are in the same direction as they were cut, and tie them back on with several pieces of kitchen string.

To make the glaze, in a small saucepan, combine the wine, sage, honey, apricots, and ½ cup (120 ml) water and bring to a boil over medium-high heat, stirring occasionally. Reduce the heat to medium and simmer until the apricots are soft and the liquid is reduced to about ½ cup (120 ml). Remove from the heat and strain through a fine-mesh sieve placed over a small heatproof bowl, pushing against the fruit with the back of a spoon to release as much liquid as possible. Reserve the liquid and discard the solids.

Place the roast, bone side down, in a large oven-safe frying pan and roast for 15 minutes. Adjust the oven control to 325°F (165°C) and continue to roast, basting five or six times with the glaze, until a meat thermometer inserted into the thickest part of the roast away from bone registers 140° to 145°F (60° to 63°C), about 45 minutes. Transfer the roast to a carving board, tent loosely with aluminum foil, and let rest for 5 to 10 minutes. While the roast rests, pit and slice the fresh apricots for garnish.

Pistachios are one of the "royal" ingredients in Iranian cuisine. Along with pomegranate seeds, saffron, and rose petals, all of which are either native to Iran or have been an integral part of the food for thousands of years, they are not only unique in flavor, but their striking color elevates an everyday dish into something out of the ordinary. Pistachios are expensive, and they are a sign to guests that a host has put money and care into a meal. They are meant to be seen, rather than ground up and hidden away inside a pastry or a thick sauce like, say, walnuts. While the distinct flavor of pistachios is a delight all its own—iconic Persian treats like gaz (nougat candy) and bastani (saffron ice cream) are unimaginable without the distinct flavor of pistachios—their bright green hue gives them an outsize impact. Pistachios are the finishing touch, tossed on top of morassa polo ("jeweled" rice) along with currants, barberries, and crystallized sugar to evoke the appearance of glowing gems, or sprinkled on shirini (bite-size sweets) before or after baking. Even one kernel of green atop a cookie is enough to transform it into something uniquely special.

—LOUISA SHAFIA, author of *The New Persian Kitchen* and creator of *Feast by Louisa*, an online Persian culinary store

To carve the roast, first snip the kitchen string and gently lift away the ribs. Carve the meat into slices either ¼ inch (6 mm) or ½ inch (12 mm) thick, depending on your preference, and arrange the slices on a warmed platter. Cut the ribs apart and add them to the platter.

Drizzle the remaining glaze over the pork slices, garnish with apricot slices and the reserved pistachios, and serve.

desserts

pistachio nut tart   Serves 8

As appealing as an old-fashioned pecan pie, this luscious tart, with its treacly pistachio filling and an extravagant topping of whole pistachios, is a nut lover's dream dessert. The crust is buttery, like shortcake, and is pressed into the pan, so no rolling required.

FOR THE PASTRY:

1⅓ cups (165 g) all-purpose flour

¼ cup (50 g) granulated sugar

4 tablespoons (55 g) cold, unsalted butter, cut into ½-inch (12-mm) chunks

1 large egg, lightly beaten

FOR THE FILLING:

¾ cup (165 g) firmly packed light brown sugar

2 large eggs

2 tablespoons unsalted butter, melted and cooled

1-inch (2.5-cm) piece vanilla bean

¾ cup (105 g) pistachios, coarsely chopped, plus ½ cup (75 g) whole pistachios

Preheat the oven to 350°F (175°C).

Make the pastry: In a bowl, stir together the flour and granulated sugar. Scatter the butter over the flour mixture and, using your fingers or a pastry blender, work in the butter until the mixture is crumbly and the consistency of coarse crumbs. Add the egg and 1 tablespoon water and stir and toss just until evenly moistened. Gather the dough into a tight ball.

Transfer the dough to 9-inch (23-cm) tart pan with a removable bottom. Using your fingers, press it firmly and evenly over the bottom and up the sides of the pan until flush with the rim. Set aside.

Make the filling: In a bowl, combine the brown sugar, eggs, and butter. Slit the vanilla bean lengthwise and scrape the seeds into the bowl. Using a whisk or a wooden spoon, beat until well blended. Stir in the chopped pistachios.

Pour the filling into the pastry-lined tart pan. Arrange the whole pistachios in a single layer on top of the filling. Cover the tart loosely with aluminum foil.

Bake the tart for 35 minutes, then remove the foil. Continue to bake until the crust and filling are golden brown, about 15 minutes longer. Let cool on a wire rack for 10 minutes. Then, using the tip of a knife, loosen the edges of the crust from the tart ring. Set the tart pan on an inverted small bowl and gently slide the tart ring downward away from the crust. Using a wide offset spatula, carefully slide the tart off the pan bottom onto a serving plate. Serve warm or at room temperature, cut into wedges. The baked tart can be stored in the refrigerator well covered or in an airtight container for up to 2 days.

lime cheesecake with pistachio crust
Makes 9 squares

Bright with the flavor of aromatic limes and grounded by a dense, rich pistachio crust, these light and airy cheesecake squares answer the call for a special-occasion dessert. Cut into smaller squares, this satisfying sweet makes a lovely addition to an afternoon tea or coffee get-together. The pistachio crust can also be used to make custard-based fruit tarts, such as blackberry or apricot.

Preheat the oven to 300°F (150°C). Line the bottom and two sides of an 8-inch (20-cm) square baking dish with a sheet of aluminum foil, pressing it in firmly and allowing a 2-inch (5-cm) overhang on both sides. Line the baking dish with a second sheet of aluminum foil in the opposite direction (perpendicular to the first sheet), again allowing a 2-inch (5-cm) overhang on both sides.

Make the crust: In a bowl, whisk together the pistachio meal, sugar, and flour until well blended. Scatter the butter over the pistachio-flour mixture and, using your fingers or a pastry blender, work in the butter until the mixture is somewhat crumbly. Gather the dough into a tight ball.

Transfer the dough to the prepared baking dish. Using your fingers, press the dough firmly and evenly onto the bottom of the dish. Set aside.

Make the filling: Set two large bowls side by side. Separate the eggs, dropping the whites into one bowl and the yolks into the second bowl.

Grate the zest from two limes and squeeze 2 tablespoons of juice into the bowl with the yolks. Add the sour cream, vanilla, sugar, flour, and salt. Using an electric mixer, beat on medium speed until smooth. Add the cream cheese, a few pieces at a time, and beat until smooth. Then add the Neufchâtel the same way, again beating until smooth.

Using clean beaters, beat the egg whites on high speed until stiff peaks form. Fold the egg whites, a little at a time, into the sour cream mixture. Pour or spoon the mixture into the prepared baking dish. Lift the baking dish and then gently tap it on the work surface to settle the filling. Using a rubber spatula, smooth the surface.

Bake the cheesecake until the center barely jiggles when the dish is shaken and a toothpick inserted into the center comes out almost clean, about 1 hour. Turn off the oven, crack the oven door, and leave the cake in the oven to cool for 1 hour longer.

Transfer the cake to a wire rack and let cool completely. Grasping the edges of the bottom layer of foil in both hands, lift the cheesecake out of the pan and place it on a work surface.

(continued)

FOR THE CRUST:

¾ cup (81 g) pistachio meal

6 tablespoons (75 g) sugar

¾ cup (95 g) all-purpose flour

4 tablespoons (55 g) cold unsalted butter, cut into ½-inch (12-mm) chunks

FOR THE FILLING:

4 large eggs

2 limes

1 cup (230 g) regular sour cream

½ teaspoon pure vanilla extract

½ cup (100 g) sugar

2 tablespoons all-purpose flour

¼ teaspoon fine sea salt

8 ounces (225 g) regular cream cheese, at room temperature, cut into 6 or 7 pieces.

8 ounces (225 g) regular Neufchâtel cheese, at room temperature, cut into 6 or 7 pieces.

FOR THE TOPPING:

½ to ⅔ cup (115 to 155 g) regular sour cream

3 thin lime slices

½ cup (70 g) pistachios, chopped

My friend Sameh Wadi is one of the most talented chefs in Minneapolis. He is an Arab American born in Kuwait of Palestinian parents whose extended family was exiled from their ancestral home. He grew up on hip-hop in South Minneapolis while learning English and staffing his father's corner grocery store.

Most evenings he eats a bowl of pistachios and thinks things through—an old habit of self-comfort. If there is not a place on earth where he can go and truly call it home, there are, on the other hand, always pistachios. "There is no Middle Eastern dessert without pistachios," he tells me, and he describes all the ways that pistachios are ground and stuffed and rolled and sprinkled and baked into almost everything he grew up thinking of as dessert.

In Arabic, the word *pistachio* means "almond from Aleppo." Yet, because of war and politics, it is almost impossible to get Syrian pistachios in the United States. Tariffs make the excellent pistachios from Iran three times more expensive than those from California, which are perfectly good but do not play any part in his childhood memories. And in this way, even the culinary homeland of pistachios is made inaccessible to him by forces out of his control.

He shows me a photo of a kind of baklava made with pistachios ground coarse, medium, and fine, then rolled up like spring rolls in layers of phyllo that, in their translucence, turn green from the filling.

"This is everything that I care about," he says.

"When will you make me some of those?" I ask.

"When I get my little hands on some of that fine Turkish pistachio powder," he says.

— STEVE J. HOFFMAN, award-winning food writer and winner of the 2019 James Beard MFK Fisher Distinguished Writing Award

lime cheesecake
with pistachio crust (continued)

Top the cake: Using a rubber spatula, spread the top of the cake evenly with the sour cream. Have ready a tall glass of hot water. Dip a sharp knife into the hot water, dry the blade, and cut the cake into 9 equal pieces, rinsing the knife in the hot water and drying it after each cut. Cut the lime slices into quarters; you'll need only 9 quarters. Garnish each cake square with a lime quarter, then sprinkle with the pistachios.

Use an offset spatula to transfer the cheesecake squares to a platter. Serve immediately, or cover loosely with plastic wrap and refrigerate for up to 2 days.

upside-down meyer lemon–pistachio cake

Serves 8 to 10

This recipe is adapted from a blood orange upside-down cake that originally appeared in Bon Appétit *magazine. Meyer lemons, sweeter than regular lemons, combined with caramel syrup and pistachios, make a versatile cake that is as perfect at teatime as it is at the conclusion of a fine meal.*

Preheat the oven to 350°F (175°C).

Combine 7 tablespoons (90 g) of the sugar and 3 tablespoons water in a 10-inch (25-cm) oven-safe frying pan with 2½-inch (6-cm) sides. Place over medium-high heat and heat, stirring occasionally, until the sugar dissolves, about 1 minute. Raise the heat to high and boil without stirring, brushing down the pan sides with a wet pastry brush as needed to release stray sugar crystals and swirling the pan occasionally so the syrup colors evenly, until the syrup is golden (not dark) amber, about 4 minutes. Remove from the heat and whisk in 2 tablespoons of the butter.

Cut off both ends of each lemon and slice the lemons into rounds ⅛ inch (3 mm) thick. Remove and discard any seeds. Top the caramel mixture with the lemon slices, arranging them in concentric circles and overlapping the slices. Sprinkle lightly with the pistachios.

In a medium bowl, whisk together the flour, polenta, baking powder, and salt until well blended. In a large bowl, using an electric mixer, beat together the ¾ cup (150 g) sugar and the remaining 6 tablespoons (85 g) butter on medium speed until well blended. Slit the vanilla bean lengthwise and scrape the seeds into the bowl. Continue to beat on medium speed until the mixture is light and fluffy. Add the egg yolks one at a time, beating well after each addition. On low speed, add the flour mixture in three batches alternately with the milk in two batches, beating just until incorporated.

Using clean beaters, beat the egg whites on medium-high speed until soft peaks form. Add the remaining 1 tablespoon sugar and continue to beat until the peaks are stiff but not dry. Using a rubber spatula, fold half of the egg whites into the batter to lighten it, then fold in the remaining whites in two batches, just until no white streaks remain. Drop the batter by large spoonfuls over the lemon slices in the pan, then spread evenly with the back of the spoon.

Bake the cake until a toothpick inserted into the center comes out clean, 35 to 45 minutes. Let cool in the pan on a wire rack for 10 minutes. Run a knife blade around the edge of the pan to loosen the cakes sides, then invert a serving platter over the pan. Using oven mitts to hold the platter and pan firmly together, invert them, allowing the cake to settle onto the platter. Adjust any lemon slices that may have become dislodged. Let the cake cool to room temperature. Cut into wedges to serve or cover loosely with plastic wrap and refrigerate for up to 2 days.

8 tablespoons (100 g) sugar, plus ¾ cup (150 g)

½ cup (115 g) unsalted butter, at room temperature, cut into 1-tablespoon slices

3 to 4 unpeeled Meyer lemons

2 tablespoons pistachios, coarsely chopped

¾ cup (95 g) plus 3 tablespoons all-purpose flour

3 tablespoons polenta

1½ teaspoons baking powder

¼ teaspoon fine sea salt

1-inch (2.5-cm) piece vanilla bean, or ¾ teaspoon pure vanilla extract

2 large eggs, separated

6 tablespoons (90 ml) whole milk

baklava with pistachios Makes about 3 dozen pieces

Baklava is a celebrated Middle Eastern dessert made with paper-thin sheets of phyllo dough, crushed nuts, and a sweet syrup. Pistachios are often the chosen nut, but walnuts are common as well. The dessert is usually prepared in a rectangular pan, then cut into diamond shapes. In this decorative change, the confection is baked in a round pan and cut into a star-shaped pattern reminiscent of traditional Middle Eastern mosaics.

In a food processor, pulse the whole pistachios until chopped to a coarse crumble. Add the cinnamon and cardamom and pulse one or two times to mix. Transfer to a bowl and set aside.

In a small saucepan, melt the butter over medium heat. Set aside off the heat.

Lay a sheet of parchment or other paper a bit larger than a 12 inch (30.5 cm) square on a work surface. Set the 12-inch (30.5-cm) round baking pan or dish you will be using for the baklava on the paper, then trace around it to make a template for cutting the phyllo dough. Cut out the circle.

Open the packages of phyllo, unfold the sheets, and lay them flat on the work surface. Count out 39 sheets, put them in a single stack, and immediately cover them with a damp kitchen towel. Fold up the remaining sheets, wrap in plastic wrap, refrigerate, and reserve for another use. Immediately, using the template and a sharp knife or scissors, cut through all the sheets to make circles to fit the pan. Cover the phyllo circles right away with a damp kitchen towel to keep them from drying out.

To assemble the baklava, brush the bottom of the baking pan or dish with plenty of the butter. Lay one circle of phyllo on the bottom and brush with butter. Repeat, brushing each layer with butter until you have a total of 8 sheets. Sprinkle about ½ cup (50 g) of the nut mixture over the phyllo. Top with 3 phyllo circles, brushing each sheet with butter, and top with about ½ cup (50 g) of the nut mixture. Repeat six more times, brushing each sheet with butter, adding about ½ cup (50 g) of the nut mixture after every 3 sheets, then finish with a final layer of 4 phyllo circles, each brushed with butter.

Using a sharp knife, cut the pastry into diamonds: Cut a diameter line through the center to divide the stack into halves. Make a second diameter line perpendicular to the first one to cut the stack into quarters. Then make two more diameter cuts to make eight triangles. Within each triangle, make 45-degree angle cuts in both directions to create diamonds.

Preheat the oven to 350°F (175°C). Bake the baklava until golden brown, about 50 minutes.

(continued)

4 cups (560 g) whole pistachios, plus 2 tablespoons chopped for garnish

½ teaspoon ground cinnamon

½ teaspoon ground cardamom

1 cup (225 g) unsalted butter

2 packages (16 ounce/455 g) phyllo dough, thawed if frozen

FOR THE SYRUP:

1 cup (200 g) sugar

½ cup (170 g) honey

1 teaspoon orange blossom water

1 teaspoon pure vanilla extract

My flight from Istanbul to Gaziantep (Antep) took a mere ninety minutes, but as our plane slowly descended toward this earthen-colored ancient city, it seemed as if we were time traveling into the past. The long descent had us skimming over endless orchards of what I later learned were pistachio trees, already heavy with a new crop.

I was on a solo food trip to the southeastern Anatolia region of Turkey, and my first stop in Gaziantep was a restaurant famous for its beef kebab seasoned with dried and crushed local chiles and served with an ice-cold metal cup of drinkable yogurt called *ayran*. For dessert, the waiter insisted I try the other dish the restaurant was famous for—baklava. I've never been a fan of this honey- sweet pastry, but what arrived was a square of flaky phyllo with a thick filling of chopped pistachios and a generous topping of ground pistachios. Its rich, nuanced flavor was the perfect balance of sweet and savory. I ordered a second piece and immediately promised myself that I would never disparage baklava again.

—JOHN McREYNOLDS, chef and author of
the award-winning *Stone Edge Farm Cookbook* and
Stone Edge Farm Kitchen Larder Cookbook

baklava with pistachios (continued)

While the baklava is baking, make the syrup: In a saucepan, combine 1 cup (240 ml) water and the sugar and bring to a boil over medium-high heat, stirring to dissolve the sugar. When the sugar has dissolved, reduce the heat to medium, add the honey and orange blossom water, and simmer, stirring occasionally, until the mixture is syrupy, about 10 minutes. Stir in the vanilla. Let cool to room temperature.

When the baklava is ready, remove it from the oven and immediately pour or spoon the room-temperature syrup over every bit of the pastry. It will soak down into the layers. Garnish with the 2 tablespoons chopped pistachios. Let cool for at least 6 hours or preferably overnight to allow the syrup to be absorbed before serving. Do not cover with plastic wrap or other covering or the baklava will become soggy. Store leftover baklava in an airtight container at room temperature in a cool place for up to 2 weeks.

Note: Because you will be cutting out 12-inch (30.5-cm) circles from the phyllo sheets, make sure to purchase phyllo sheets that are at least 13 inches (33 cm) long and wide. You will need 39 sheets to assemble the baklava. Most phyllo packages carry 20 or 24 sheets, so plan on buying two packages.

ABOVE: *In Turkey, large, decorative trays of handmade baklava in many styles are sold in markets throughout the country.*

plums with pistachio crème anglaise

Serves 4

Crème anglaise, that sweet creamy custard sauce so beloved by the French, is given a fanciful twist with the addition of pistachio paste, a simple concoction of finely ground pistachios and sugar (see page 47). It makes the perfect accompaniment to ruby-colored roasted plums in summer and early fall.

Preheat the oven to 400°F (200°C).

Roast the plums: Rub the plum halves all over with the oil. Arrange them, cut side up, in a baking dish just large enough to hold them. Sprinkle evenly with the sugar.

Roast the plums until juice is just beginning to collect in the pan and their surface is shiny, about 15 minutes. Set aside until ready to serve.

Make the crème anglaise: In a bowl, whisk together the egg yolks and sugar until the mixture is pale yellow, about 1 minute. Set aside.

In a saucepan, heat the cream over medium-high heat just until small bubbles appear around the edge of the pan. Remove from the heat. Pour about one-fourth of the hot cream into the egg mixture while whisking constantly. Pour the egg-cream mixture into the cream remaining in the pan and set over medium heat. Using a wooden spoon, stir until the sauce is thick enough to coat the back of the spoon, about 5 minutes. Add the pistachio paste and stir until fully incorporated.

Remove from the heat and stir in the vanilla. Pour the sauce through a fine-mesh sieve placed over a small heatproof bowl. Cover with plastic wrap, pressing it directly onto the surface to prevent a film from forming, until ready to serve, or store in the refrigerator for up to 1 day.

To serve, bring the custard to room temperature if it has been refrigerated. Spoon a pool of the crème anglaise onto the bottom of four dessert bowls or plates. Add 2 plum halves, cut side up, to each serving. Sprinkle with the pistachios and serve any remaining crème anglaise on the side.

FOR THE PLUMS:

4 ripe purple plums, halved and pitted

2 tablespoons extra-virgin olive oil

2 tablespoons sugar

FOR THE CRÈME ANGLAISE:

4 large egg yolks

⅓ cup (65 g) sugar

1 cup (240 ml) heavy cream

3 tablespoons pistachio paste

½ teaspoon pure vanilla extract

½ cup (70 g) pistachios, chopped, for garnish

roasted peaches topped with pistachio paste and crumble Serves 4

These warm, juicy peaches filled with pistachio paste and topped with a buttery pistachio crumble recall the flavors of peach cobbler but without the pastry crust. Easy to assemble and prepare, they are best enjoyed straight from the oven, preferably served with soft whipped cream or a little vanilla or pistachio ice cream (see page 140).

Preheat the oven to 425°F (220°C).

Brush the cut sides of the peach halves with the oil and sprinkle evenly with 3 tablespoons of the sugar.

Depending on how many peach halves you are working with, divide the pistachio paste into 4 or 8 portions and, with your hands, roll each portion into a ball. Fit each peach cavity with a ball, flattening it slightly to fit the cavity but leaving it mounded.

In a small bowl, combine the nuts, flour, 2 tablespoons of the sugar, and the butter. Using a fork, mix the ingredients together to create a crumbly mixture.

Arrange the filled peach halves, cut side up, in a baking dish just large enough to hold them and sprinkle with the nut mixture. Roast the peaches until they are soft and juicy, the surface is lightly glazed, and the nut crumble is lightly browned, about 15 minutes.

While the peaches are roasting, in a bowl, using an electric mixer, whip together the cream and the remaining ½ tablespoon sugar on medium-high speed until soft peaks form.

When the peaches are ready, divide them evenly, filling side up, among four dessert bowls or plates. Add a dollop of the whipped cream to each serving and serve immediately.

2 large or 4 small, ripe freestone peaches, halved and pitted

2 tablespoons pistachio oil

5½ tablespoons (70 g) sugar, plus more if needed

½ cup (125 g) pistachio paste

½ cup (70 g) pistachios, finely chopped

2 tablespoons all-purpose flour

2 tablespoons unsalted butter, cut into small pieces

½ cup (120 ml) heavy cream

pistachio ice cream sandwiches

Makes 2 quarts (2 l) ice cream; 12 ice cream sandwiches

Homemade pistachio ice cream is a treat that everyone will enjoy. To increase the fun, make ice cream sandwiches garnished with toasted pistachios. Once the sandwiches are made, they can be individually wrapped and frozen, ready to be handed out on a hot summer day.

FOR THE ICE CREAM:

2½ cups (600 ml) whole milk

1 cup (200 g) sugar

1 cup (240 ml) half-and-half

1 teaspoon pure almond extract

1 teaspoon pure vanilla extract

¾ cup (190 g) pistachio paste

1 cup (140 g) pistachios, coarsely chopped

24 chocolate wafer or shortbread cookies, about 2 inches (5 cm) in diameter

1 cup (140 g) pistachios, toasted and coarsely chopped, for garnish

In a saucepan, heat the milk over medium-high just until small bubbles appear around the edge of the pan. Add the sugar and stir until dissolved. Add the half-and-half, almond and vanilla extracts, and pistachio paste and stir until the paste is well blended. Reduce the heat to low and simmer, stirring frequently, for 5 minutes.

Remove from the heat and pour into a heatproof bowl. Let cool until tepid, then cover and refrigerate for at least 4 hours or up to overnight.

Stir the untoasted nuts into the chilled custard, then pour the custard into an ice cream maker and freeze according to the manufacturer's instructions.

While the ice cream is churning, line the bottom and sides of a 9 by 5-inch (23 by 13-cm) loaf pan with two sheets of aluminum foil, one lengthwise and one crosswise and each piece with a 2-inch (5-cm) overhang. Once the ice cream is frozen, pack it into the lined pan, cover the top with the foil overhang, and place in the freezer until ready to use. It will keep for up to 1 month.

To make the sandwiches, line up 12 of the cookies, bottom side up, on a work surface. Put the toasted nuts on a flat plate. Unmold the ice cream by grasping the foil overhang, lifting it out of the pan, and then inverting it onto a sheet pan. Peel away the foil liner and return it to the pan.

Working quickly, cut a slice 1 inch (2.5 cm) thick from one end of the block. Using a 2-inch (5-cm) round biscuit or cookie cutter, cut the slice into 2 rounds. Working quickly, scoop up the ice cream scraps, press them back onto the ice cream block, cover the top with the foil, and return to the freezer. Place each ice cream round on an overturned cookie and top with a second cookie, bottom side down, to make a sandwich. Roll the sides of each sandwich in the toasted pistachios, pressing gently so they adhere. Wrap each sandwich separately in foil and place in the freezer.

Repeat the process five more times to make 12 ice cream sandwiches total, always pressing any scraps onto the ice cream block and returning it to the freezer after cutting each slice. The sandwiches will keep for up to 1 month.

afghan rose water–flavored pudding with pistachio, strawberry, and rose petal topping

Serves 4

As delicate and ethereal as a mist over the desert, this silky pudding is a traditional dessert in Afghanistan, where it is flavored with rose water and pistachios. Here, rosy fresh strawberries and dried rose petals have been added, making the chilled dessert a festive and fragrant complement to nearly any menu. Be sure to use rose water, not rose water extract, which is much stronger.

In a saucepan, heat the milk over medium-high heat just until small bubbles begin to appear around the edge of the pan. Remove from the heat. In a small bowl, whisk together the cornstarch and 3 tablespoons of the hot milk. Whisk the cornstarch mixture into the pan of hot milk, then whisk in the sugar and rose water. Return the pan to medium-low and heat, stirring, just until the mixture starts to thicken a little, 4 to 6 minutes.

Divide the pudding evenly among four ¾-cup (180-ml) serving glasses. Cover with plastic wrap, pressing it directly onto the surface of the pudding to prevent a film from forming. Refrigerate until chilled, at least 2 hours or up to overnight.

Put the berries into a bowl, drizzle with the honey, and turn gently. The berries can be prepared up to 6 hours in advance, covered, and refrigerated.

When ready to serve, uncover the serving glasses and, using a fork, scrape the surface of the puddings a bit. Sprinkle the puddings evenly with half of the pistachios, then top each pudding with one-fourth of the strawberries and their juices and one-fourth of the rose petals. Finish with a sprinkle of the remaining nuts. Serve immediately.

2 cups (480 ml) whole milk

3 tablespoons cornstarch

1 cup (200 g) sugar

1 teaspoon rose water

1½ cups (215 g) strawberries, hulled and thinly sliced

2 tablespoons honey

4 tablespoons (25 g) finely chopped pistachios

1 cup (28 g) culinary-grade dried rose petals

classic sicilian cannoli with pistachios

Makes about 20 cannoli

FOR THE SHELLS:

Grapeseed or canola oil, for the molds and for deep-frying

2 cups (250 g) all-purpose flour, plus more for dusting

1 tablespoon granulated sugar

⅛ teaspoon fine sea salt

1½ tablespoons unsalted butter, cut into pieces

1 large egg yolk

¾ cup (180 ml) sweet Marsala or white wine

1 large egg beaten with 1 tablespoon water

FOR THE FILLING:

2 cups (480 g) whole-milk ricotta cheese, drained in a fine-mesh sieve for 8 hours or longer, up to 24 hours if it is very wet.

1 cup (120 g) confectioners' sugar, plus more for garnish

Freshly grated zest of ½ orange

½ to ¾ cup (70 g to 105 g) pistachios, toasted and finely chopped

½ cup (80 g) drained Amarena cherries, chopped (optional)

Sicily is famous for its cannoli, but the crispy shells filled with sweetened ricotta are eaten elsewhere in Italy and almost anywhere there's an Italian bakery. Some versions include chocolate chips, cinnamon or other spices, citrus zest, or candied cherries. This version focuses on pistachios, with a little orange zest added and optional cherries. Once you have the cannoli molds, the pastry shells are surprisingly easy to make, and using a pastry bag makes filling them a snap.

To make the cannoli shells, rub the outside of 12 cannoli molds with some of the oil. In a bowl, whisk together the flour, granulated sugar, and salt. Scatter the butter over the flour mixture and, using your fingers or a pastry blender, work in the butter until the mixture feels sandy. With a wooden spoon, beat in the egg yolk, then add the Marsala until a smooth dough forms. Gather the dough into a ball, wrap it in plastic wrap, and refrigerate for 1 hour.

While the dough chills, make the filling: In a bowl, combine the ricotta and confectioners' sugar and mix well with a whisk or wooden spoon. Stir in the orange zest, ¼ cup (25 g) of the pistachios, and the cherries, if using. Cover and refrigerate while preparing the shells.

Flour a work surface and place the dough on it. Pat the dough into a disk about 1 inch (2.5 cm) thick and then sprinkle with a little flour. Using a rolling pin, roll out the dough as thinly as you can, ideally at least ⅛ inch (3 mm) thick. The thinner the dough, the crunchier the shells will be. Using a 3½- to 4-inch (9- to 10-cm) round cookie or biscuit cutter (or an overturned glass), cut the dough into rounds. You should have about 20 rounds.

Wrap a round of dough lengthwise around a mold, overlapping the edges slightly. Brush the underside of the overlap with a little of the egg-water mixture, then press the overlap to seal. Set the mold, seam side up, on a sheet pan. Repeat until all the molds have been wrapped. Cover the remaining rounds with a slightly damp kitchen towel to prevent drying.

Pour the oil to a depth of 2 inches (5 cm) into large, deep pot and heat to 350°F (175°C) on a deep-frying thermometer. Line a second sheet pan with paper towels and set it near the stove.

When the oil is hot, using tongs, grip a mold and gently drop into the oil. Add another mold or two, being careful not to crowd the pan. Fry the shells, turning them gently with the tongs, until golden and crispy, 2 to 3 minutes. When they are ready, transfer them to the sheet pan.

(continued)

Although some sources claim the pistachio arrived in Italy with either Greeks or North Africans in the first millennium, records show that the red Cerasola variety was introduced into Italy from Syria in 30 CE by the Romans.

Today, there are several pistachio varieties in Italy, but the most prevalent is the *Pistacia vera*, grown in Sicily—specifically, the provinces of Agrigento and Catania—and protected by the Protected Designation of Origin (DOP) certification. There are new orchards being developed on the mainland of Italy in Basilicata and experimental crops in Tuscany. Recent Italian production has risen to nearly three thousand tons annually, making Italy the world's seventh largest producer.

The most "famous" pistachios come from the village of Bronte, near Catania, on the west side of Mount Etna, the tallest active European volcano. The fertile land around Etna produces irresistible tomatoes, blood oranges, prickly pears, wine grapes, and especially pistachios.

Sicilian pistachios are sweet and buttery and are primarily used in sweets, although many creative chefs are finding new expressions for them in savory dishes such as tossing them with pasta, or encrusting fish or poultry fillets in meal or finely ground flour. In northern Italy, the cured sausage, mortadella of Bologna, is often studded with pistachios. Most gelaterie in Italy offer pistachio gelato, and the most authentic recipe can be identified by the color—a soft, pale green.

—PAMELA SHELDON JOHNS, award-winning author of sixteen cookbooks, including *Sicily*, and founder of Food Artisans culinary tours; www.foodartisans.com

classic sicilian cannoli with pistachios (continued)

Using the tongs to hold a mold with one hand, use a kitchen towel or oven mitt in your other hand to gently slide the shell off the mold. Place the shell on the towel-lined sheet pan to cool. Repeat with the remaining fried shells, then repeat until the dough-wrapped molds have been fried and then the remaining rounds have been shaped and fried. (Note: The molds cool off quickly for reuse.) Let the fried shells cool completely before filling. They can be fried up to 6 hours in advance and left uncovered at room temperature.

When ready to serve, spoon the chilled filling into a piping bag fitted with a large star or round tip. Pipe the filling into the shells, working from both ends to ensure it reaches the center and filling each end to the edge. (Or use a plastic bag with a corner snipped off or a small spoon to fill the shells.) Sprinkle both ends with the pistachios and set the cannoli on a platter.

When all the cannoli are filled, dust lightly with confectioners' sugar and serve immediately. If filled and left to sit, the shells will become soggy.

pistachio financiers   Makes 12 cakes

Buttery and moist on the inside, crispy on the outside, these little French cakes are most often served with after-dinner coffee or as one of a selection of mignardises, small, bite-size sweets served after the main dessert. However, they are also good with morning coffee, afternoon tea, or anytime you want a sweet. Sometimes they're garnished with candied cherries or with bits of almond or pistachios, as they are here. They are easy to make and can be spooned into molds of varied sizes and shapes, such as miniature loaf pans, madeleine pans, oval boats, and rounds. Here, a standard muffin pan with ½-cup (120-ml) cups is used to bake a dozen little, round cakes.

Preheat the oven to 350°F (175°C). Liberally coat the cups of a 12-cup standard muffin pan with the 1 tablespoon room-temperature butter, carefully applying it all the way to the edge of each cup rim and using more butter if necessary. This will ensure the cakes have the characteristic crispy exterior.

In a small saucepan, melt the remaining ½ cup (115 g) butter over medium-low heat until brown bits form (the toasted milk solids) and the butter makes a bubbling sound and smells nutty, about 10 minutes. Be careful it does not burn. Remove from the heat and pour into a small heat-proof bowl. Let stand until the clear liquid and brown bits have separated.

In a spice grinder or a small food processor, grind the whole pistachios until reduced to a coarse-ground meal. Transfer to a bowl, add the flour, confectioners' sugar, and baking powder, and whisk together until well blended.

In a second bowl, using an electric mixer, beat together the egg whites, granulated sugar, and salt on medium speed just until blended, about 30 seconds.

Add one-third of the egg white mixture to the flour mixture and whisk to blend. Repeat with the remaining egg white mixture in two batches, whisking well after each addition. Then pour in the butter, leaving the brown bits behind in the bowl (it is fine if some sneak in), and whisk again until well blended.

Fill each prepared cup half full with the batter and sprinkle with the chopped pistachios, dividing them evenly.

Bake the cakes until the tops are browned and the sides are pulling away from the edge of the cups, 10 to 12 minutes. Let cool in the pan on a wire rack for 10 minutes, then remove the cakes from the pan, using the tip of a knife if needed to release them.

Serve the cakes warm or at room temperature. Once they are cool, they can be put into an airtight container and stored at room temperature for up to 5 days or frozen for up to 2 months.

½ cup (115 g) unsalted butter, plus 1 tablespoon, at room temperature

½ cup (70 g) whole pistachios, plus ¼ cup (30 g) coarsely chopped

½ cup (65 g) all-purpose flour

1 cup (120 g) confectioners' sugar

1 teaspoon baking powder

5 large egg whites

1½ tablespoons granulated sugar

⅛ teaspoon fine sea salt

Red Lips and Stained Hands

When two enterprising young brothers from Syria immigrated to America in 1912, they had a dream: to bring a taste of their homeland to their new country. Among the delicacies Frank and John Germack imported were pistachios, a favorite among the growing number of Turkish, Greek, and Middle Eastern immigrants. Back home, harvesting methods did not require pistachios to be hulled and washed immediately. As a result, natural chemicals from the nut's outer husk could cause stains on the shells, making the nuts less appealing to the uninitiated pistachio consumer in the United States.

Frank had the idea to dye the nuts bright red to improve the shell aesthetic and attract new customers. The red-dyed pistachios became wildly popular and were quickly a hallmark of the Germacks' Detroit-based company. The brothers branded their successful new product "Red Lip" in their packaging and promotions.

When California began growing pistachios in the mid-1970s, removing the husk within twenty-four hours became standard practice, eliminating the problem of stained shells. With the rapid growth in the US pistachio crop, the natural pale beige shell eventually won out. But the Germack Pistachio Company still offers red-dyed pistachios, which are now labeled "Holiday Red" and are popular at Christmastime.

— BLAKE HALLANAN, journalist

chocolate-pistachio raspberry bars

Makes 18 bars

Dense and thick like brownies, these special dessert bars combine tangy raspberries and chocolate with the delicate flavor and crunch of pistachios. The two brilliantly colored toppings—finely ground green pistachios and dried pink rose petals—were inspired by Australian cookbook author Donna Hay. Here, they sit atop a luscious chocolate frosting.

Preheat the oven to 350°F (175°C).

Make the bars: Grease the bottom and sides of an 8-inch (20-cm) square baking pan with butter. Cut a length of parchment paper the width of the pan and long enough to line the bottom and overhang two sides by at least 2 inches (5 cm). Press the parchment into the pan.

In a saucepan, melt the butter over low heat. Add the granulated sugar and stir just until mixed. Remove from the heat and pour the mixture into a heatproof bowl. Let cool slightly, about 5 minutes. Add the eggs one at a time, stirring well after each addition. Add the vanilla and stir to mix well. Add the cocoa powder, flour, and salt and stir just until mixed. Finally, stir in the raspberries and pistachios.

Using a rubber spatula, spread the batter evenly in the prepared pan and smooth the surface. Bake until a toothpick inserted into the center comes out clean, about 30 minutes.

While the cake is baking, make the frosting: In a bowl, using a wooden spoon or an electric mixer on medium speed, cream together the butter and confectioners' sugar until a smooth paste forms. Repeat while adding the cocoa. Add the milk and vanilla extract to achieve a spreadable frosting. If the frosting is too stiff, add a little more milk.

When the cake is ready, remove from the oven. Gently lift the edges of the parchment and carefully invert the cake onto a platter or small sheet pan. Peel away the parchment.

Using an offset spatula, cover the top of the cake with the frosting. Then, using a knife, draw a light line down the center of the frosted cake. Sprinkle a layer of the rose petals on one half; they will not cover it completely. Cover the other half with the pistachios in a solid layer. Cover loosely with plastic wrap and refrigerate until chilled, about 1 hour.

When ready to serve, remove from the refrigerator and cut the cake in half between the two toppings. Cut each half into bars about 1½ inches by 3 inches (4 cm by 7.5 cm). The bars will keep in an airtight container in the refrigerator for up to 1 week. Let them come to room temperature before serving.

FOR THE BARS:

½ cup (115 g) unsalted butter, plus more for the pan

1¼ cups (250 g) granulated sugar

2 large eggs

1 teaspoon pure vanilla extract

¾ cup (65 g) unsweetened cocoa powder

½ cup (60 g) all-purpose flour

¼ teaspoon fine sea salt

1 cup (20 g) freeze-dried raspberries

½ cup (70 g) pistachios, coarsely chopped

FOR THE FROSTING:

4 tablespoons (55 g) unsalted butter, at room temperature

1½ cups (180 g) confectioners' sugar

¼ cup (20 g) unsweetened cocoa powder

2½ tablespoons whole milk, plus more if needed

1 teaspoon pure vanilla extract

FOR THE TOPPING:

½ cup (14 g) culinary-grade dried rose petals, crushed

½ cup (70 g) pistachios, finely ground

pistachio cookies with candied cherries

Makes about 30 cookies

These little thumbprint cookies, made with a combination of ground pistachios and all-purpose flour, are rich but not overly sweet. The festive colors of the red cherries and green pistachios make them ideal for the holidays and the perfect addition to a seasonal cookie gift box.

1 cup (225 g) unsalted butter, at room temperature

⅔ cup (135 g) sugar

2 large egg yolks

½ teaspoon fine sea salt

1 teaspoon pure vanilla or almond extract (optional)

¾ cup (105 g) pistachios, finely ground

2½ cups (310 g) all-purpose flour

4 ounces (115 g) whole candied cherries, halved

30 whole pistachios, toasted, for garnish

In a bowl, using an electric mixer, beat the butter on medium speed until soft and fluffy, stopping to scrape down the sides of the bowl as needed. Add the sugar and continue to beat until light and fluffy. Add the egg yolks, salt, and vanilla extract (if using) and beat on medium speed until well blended.

On low speed, add ½ cup (70 g) of the nuts and the flour and beat until a dough forms and begins to stick together. Remove the dough from the bowl and press it together, turning it several times to make sure all the ingredients are evenly blended. Form the dough into a ball, wrap in plastic wrap, and refrigerate for at least 1 hour or up to overnight.

Preheat the oven to 350°F (175°C). Line a sheet pan with parchment paper.

Spread the remaining nuts on a small, flat plate. To shape the cookies, tear off a walnut-size piece from the dough ball and roll between your palms to make a 1-inch (2.5-cm) ball. Gently press the top of each ball into the nuts and then place the balls, nut side up, on the prepared sheet pan, spacing them about 2 inches (5 cm) apart.

Bake the cookies until lightly golden, about 7 minutes. Remove from the oven and, with the end of a wooden spoon, gently make an indentation in the center of each cookie. Return to the oven and continue to bake until golden, 7 to 8 minutes longer. Transfer the pan to a wire rack. While the cookies are still warm, gently press a candied cherry half and a whole pistachio into each indentation. Then transfer the cookies to the wire rack and let cool completely before serving.

To store the cookies, layer them in an airtight container, separating the layers with parchment or waxed paper, and keep at room temperature for up to 1 week.

pistachio-strawberry meringues

Makes 10 to 12 meringues; serves 5 or 6

An old-fashioned dessert, meringues are making a comeback thanks to innovative chefs who are experimenting with a variety of flavors and toppings. Here, they are dressed up with pistachios and strawberries. For an even more elaborate dessert, accompany each serving with a scoop of pistachio ice cream (see page 140) or a dollop of whipped cream.

Preheat the oven to 250°F (120°C). Line a large sheet pan with parchment paper.

In a large bowl, using an electric mixer, beat together the egg whites, cream of tartar, salt, and vanilla on medium-high speed until soft peaks form. Gradually add the 1½ cups (300 g) sugar, a few tablespoons at a time, beating after each addition until stiff, glossy peaks form. Beat in the pistachio meal.

Scoop up about ¾ cup (180 ml) of the egg-white mixture and drop it onto the prepared sheet pan in a mound about 3 inches (7.5 cm) in diameter. Using the back of a spoon, shape a shallow well in the center of the mound. Repeat, using the remaining mixture to make a total of 10 to 12 meringues.

Bake the meringues for 1 hour. Turn off the oven and leave the meringues to cool in the closed oven for at least 2 hours or up to overnight. To store the meringues until ready to use, layer them in an airtight container, separating the layers with parchment or waxed paper, and keep at room temperature for up to 4 days.

Cut the strawberries into halves or quarters, if large, and leave the small ones whole. Place in a bowl, sprinkle with the remaining 2 tablespoons sugar, and toss gently to coat evenly. Cover and refrigerate until ready to use.

To serve, place 2 meringues on each dessert plate. Spoon some of the strawberries and their juice onto each meringue. Sprinkle with the chopped pistachios and garnish with the mint, if using. Serve immediately.

6 large egg whites

1½ teaspoons cream of tartar

⅛ teaspoon fine sea salt

1 teaspoon pure vanilla extract

1½ cups (300 g) plus 2 tablespoons sugar

3 tablespoons pistachio meal

4 cups (575 g) strawberries, hulled

¼ cup (35 g) pistachios, chopped

Fresh mint or lemon verbena leaves, for garnish (optional)

dark chocolate pistachio bark

Makes about 12 ounces (340 g); serves 6

This beautiful bark, subtly flavored with cardamom and finished with sea salt, is quick and easy to make, even for a novice. It stores well in the refrigerator, ready to bring out for a snack or to conclude a meal. It also makes a special holiday gift.

1 tablespoon unsalted butter

2 cups (340 g) semisweet chocolate chips

¾ cup (105 g) whole pistachios, toasted

¾ cup (105 g) whole pistachios, coarsely chopped, plus 2 table-spoons finely chopped

½ teaspoon ground cardamom

2 teaspoons flaky sea salt, such as Maldon

Grease the bottom of a large sheet pan with the butter, then line it with parchment paper.

Pour water to a depth of 1 inch (2.5 cm) into the bottom of a double boiler and replace the top pan. (Or use a medium saucepan and a heatproof bowl that fits snugly in its rim.) Place over medium heat. When the water begins to simmer, add the chocolate to the top pan (or bowl) and stir as it melts. When it is fully melted, remove from over the water and stir the whole toasted pistachios, coarsely chopped pistachios, and the cardamom into the chocolate, mixing well.

Pour the chocolate mixture onto the prepared sheet pan. Using a rubber spatula, spread it into a rectangle about ¼ inch (6 mm) thick. Sprinkle evenly with the salt and the finely chopped pistachios and gently press them into the chocolate. Refrigerate until firm, at least 2 hours or up to 8 hours.

To serve, break the bark into irregular pieces by hand or with a knife. To store, layer the pieces in an airtight container, separating the layers with parchment or waxed paper, and refrigerate for up to 1 month.

acknowledgments

While considering a third book on nuts following *Almonds: Recipes, History, Culture* and *Pecans: Recipes & History of an American Nut*, one thing became clear about pistachios: these tiny gems are finally getting their deserved attention in kitchens around the globe. I was fortunate to assemble a talented project team for this book, including Jennifer Barry, whose design talent and vision are on par with her masterful collaborative abilities; Robert Holmes, whose visual artistry shines in both the recipe photography and images of the beautiful pistachio orchards and their harvest, supported by Andrea Johnson; and Georgeanne Brennan, whose inspired recipes deliciously embrace the sweet and savory dimensions of the pistachio. Edward Whealon was invaluable as the project coordinator from St. Louis, and I am deeply grateful for all his hard work and managerial talents.

We couldn't have brought the glorious pistachio nut to life in these pages without the help of some generous California growers and resources. Teresa Keenan and the Keenan family supplied us with pistachios for our recipes and photography and allowed us to photograph their orchards, from bud to harvest, at Keenan Farms. Our gratitude also goes out to Richard Matoian, President of American Pistachio Growers, Richard Grotjahn, and Shelby Mitchell of Santa Barbara Pistachio Company for allowing us to photograph pistachio farms in other parts of the Golden State. K.C. Loquaci Cornwell and CA Grown graciously helped connect us to the welcoming California pistachio growers who are featured in our book.

We are thrilled to have published this book with Cameron + Company and are deeply grateful to publisher Chris Gruener and editorial director Pippa White, who championed our project at Abrams Books. They, along with Cameron's creative director Iain Morris and managing editor Jan Hughes, helped guide our efforts along the way. Cookbook authors Pamela Sheldon Johns and Cenk Sönmezsoy connected us to some of our wonderful sidebar contributors. And Matthieu Kohlmeyer and Karnika Haridoss of La Tourangelle embraced our promotional ideas to highlight their wonderful pistachio oil in many of the recipes.

My friends Andy Kim and chef/restaurateur Ben Poremba launched us on our pistachio adventure, for which I'm deeply grateful. Betsy Fentress, my cohort on so many projects, provided constant encouragement and guidance along the way. Among all my friends who supported me, I owe a special thank you to those who used my book to raise money for the charities close to my heart.

Lastly, to my children and their spouses, Derek, Jamie, Christina, Thomas, Justin, and Kelly, and my six grandchildren, Lilly, Rosemary, France, Jax, Ladd, and Luke, three of whom were born while I was working on this book. I could not do this without your love and support.

—Barbara Bryant

When Barbara Bryant and book producer Jenny Barry approached me to participate in this book, I jumped at the chance to explore and expand the many culinary possibilities of pistachios. First and foremost, my thanks go out to them for inviting me into the pistachio tent. I am grateful to my family and to my friends, especially Ann M. Evans, Margie Olson, and Dave and Judy Gilchrist, who spent long days in my kitchen patiently helping me test the recipes for the book. In addition to testing and tasting, my husband, Jim Schrupp, washed more pots and pans than he wants to remember. Thanks also to the local Schrupp families, the faithful recipe tasters who were always happy to try every new idea I proposed and appreciated the results after a long day of cooking.

A very special thank you goes to Kim Kissling and her assistant, Becca Martin, who did such a spectacular job of cooking and styling the dishes for the book, and to Ethel Brennan, my daughter and prop stylist, who selected and provided the vast array of tableware that enhanced the brilliant photography of Robert Holmes. No book is complete without good project editors, and I am grateful to have had the discerning Blake Hallanan on the team as well as my longtime copy editor and colleague, Sharon Silva.   —Georgeanne Brennan

index

photography credits

ABOVE: *Pistachio ice cream is popular around the world. A woman in Oaxaca, Mexico, enjoys an afternoon cone.*

Alamy Stock Photo
Page 19: Danita Delimont (middle left), Prisma by Dukas Presseagentur GmbH (middle right), blickwinkel (bottom left); page 32: Irina Naoumova (top left), Reuters (middle left), Alex Ramsay (middle right), Jon Arnold Images Ltd (bottom left), Reuters (bottom right); page 33: Wead; page 45: Mehmet Doruk Tasci Resul; page 136: Resul Muslu

Andrea Johnson
Page 18; page 20; page 24 (middle left); page 29 (top right, bottom left, and bottom right); pages 30–31

Bridgeman Images
Page 11: illustration by Pierre Jean Francois Turpin, © NPL De Agostini Picture Library/ Bridgeman Images

Getty Images
Page 19: (bottom right) Siculodoc/iStock; page 32: (top right) Siculodoc/iStock; page 146: EyesWideOpen/Getty Images News

Masood Khezri
Page 24: (top left and top right)

Shutterstock
Page 34: © 2021 Georgios Tsichlis/Shutterstock